Paul Ferrini's work is a must read take responsibility fo.

JOHN BRADSHAW

Paul Ferrini's books are the most important I have read. I study them like a Bible.

ELISABETH KÜBLER-ROSS

Paul Ferrini's writing will inspire you to greater insights and understandings, to more clarity and a grander resolve to make changes in your life that can truly change the world.

NEALE DONALD WALSCH

Paul Ferrini is an important teacher in the new millenium. Reading his work has been a major awakening for me.

IYANLA VANZANT

Paul Ferrini is a modern day Kahlil Gibran — poet, mystic, visionary, teller of truth.

LARRY DOSSEY

I feel that this work comes from a continuous friendship with the deepest Part of the Self. I trust its wisdom.

COLEMAN BARKS

Paul Ferrini reconnects us to the Spirit Within, to that place where even our deepest wounds can be healed.

JOAN BORYSENKO

Paul Ferrini's wonderful books show us a way to walk lightly with joy on planet Earth.

GERALD JAMPOLSKY

Please visit our website for more information:
www.paulferrini.com
www.lightforthesoul.com

ISBN # 978-1-879159-97-6

Library of Congress Control Number: 2016921081

Manufactured in the United States of America

Answering the Call of the Soul

How Suffering Transforms Our Consciousness and Our Experience of the World

Paul Ferrini

TABLE OF CONTENTS

PREFACE
by Khadra Sufi

There is this song from R. Kelly, *"The storm is over now."* Years ago, when I heard it for the first time, I started crying. Tears of frustration came out because he was singing about release from pain. He was singing about the end of fear and suffering. He was singing the words that my heart wanted to hear:

> "The storm is over now
> And I can see the sunshine
> (Somewhere beyond the clouds)
> I feel Heaven, yeah
> (Heaven is over me)."

I wanted so badly to believe those words, but I just couldn't. Everything in my life felt so dark and hopeless. I was in a downward spin, sinking into the pit of self-loathing and despair.

All I wanted was someone who was there for me, to hold me and protect me, but I kept pushing everyone away.

I kept running away from facing the deep wounds that came from my childhood growing up in Somalia.

I had to sit for a very long time in the darkest corners of my fear and I had to sit there alone.

"Why would God do this to me?" I kept asking. "Why would He punish me and leave me alone?"

It took me a long time to find the light in my dark night of the soul. In time, I began to realize that God had not abandoned me. He was calling out to me, asking me to take the journey of healing step by step. He knew my strength and he trusted me to realize my higher potential.

As I slowly moved forward my thinking began to change. I began to see myself as God's child, instead of as a victim who was being punished.

Like many people, I thought I needed a relationship with a man, a great job, and a big income to realize my power and potential. But while I was able to create all of that at one time or another, none of it really satisfied me. I still was unhappy inside.

One day I read a book by Paul Ferrini called "*Love Without Conditions.*" The book touched me deeply. It helped me to look at my wounds and move through my shame. It helped me to find forgiveness for myself and others. Then I was able to begin the process of learning to love myself unconditionally.

Today, I am closer to that than ever before, but sometimes the old fears come up and I feel full of shame and unworthiness. Then, I have to go back into the pain and deepen my healing.

I know that this is not a punishment, but an invitation to grow, to become stronger and to begin to trust myself and to trust God at a deeper level.

I asked Paul to write this book as a reminder to me and to you that we are not here to be punished or to suffer without purpose or hope in the future. As Paul says, "suffering can be a doorway to truth and transformation. It is part of our evolutionary process to forgive, to heal, and to become whole again."

In *Love Without Conditions*, Jesus tells us "I am the door to love without conditions. When you walk through you too will be the door."

Our healing and empowerment is the proof to all of our brothers and sisters that transformation is possible. As you read through the pages of this amazing book you will know, as I do, that your true greatness lies on the other side of your pain.

Then, we can all look up and see the mountains and the sky. Then we can all know in our hearts that "the storm is over."

Khadra Sufi

Answering the Call
of the Soul

People will do anything, no matter how absurd,

to avoid facing their own soul....

Who looks outside, dreams;

who looks inside, awakes.

C.G. JUNG

For Khadra
Who Asked for This Book

INTRODUCTION

Suffering can be a doorway to truth and transformation.
It is part of our evolutionary process to forgive,
to heal, and to become whole again.

When my friend Khadra asked me "Why do we suffer?" I answered, "We suffer in part because we have
something to learn. Something in us needs to soften and
become more humble. Something in us needs to learn to be
more compassionate toward ourselves and others."

That aspect of our suffering is non-negotiable. We
aren't going to be able to deny or blow off our lessons.
Sooner or later, we have to learn them. However, being a
willing learner makes it much easier for us to move through
our pain into our empowerment.

In that sense, pain is not necessarily a bad thing. It can
serve a purpose. It can be a wake-up call that tells us that

something in our lives needs to shift so that we can come back into balance.

However, there is a layer of our pain and suffering that results from our resistance to our life lessons, from our refusal to soften and learn, and we can do something about that. We can see our resistance and move through it. We can stop being a victim and learn what life is trying to teach us.

Much of our suffering is caused by repetitive patterns of self-betrayal resulting from our childhood wounds. Bringing our wounds to the surface so that they can be healed is an important part of our psychospiritual journey of integration. We all need to understand and dismantle the blocks to love in our hearts. We all need to understand and transcend our reactive patterns of fight, flight, or emotional shutdown.

So, if we do our spiritual work, many of the root causes of our suffering can be neutralized. That is the good news. The bad news is that if we don't do our spiritual work, our suffering will intensify.

The choice is ours to make. Some of us heed the message the first time the messenger comes to our door. Others procrastinate, hoping the messenger will go away.

That is wishful thinking. Today, the messenger may come dressed as a therapist or a teacher. Next week he may come with a company of soldiers wielding a battering ram. When that happens, we have no choice but to open the door.

Some of us are willing learners. Some of us must be driven onto our knees before we heed the call and reach out for help.

TWO TYPES OF PEOPLE

There are two types of people here on planet earth: those who feel their pain and those who don't. Those who feel their pain tend to be able to feel the pain of others. Those who don't feel their pain tend to have difficulty feeling the pain of others.

The challenge for those who feel their pain is not to become identified with it. They need to learn that while they may have pain, they are not their pain. If they identify with their pain and the pain of others, they will get stuck in it. They will live their lives as victims and give their power away to others. They will feel powerless to make the changes in their lives that are necessary for their own growth and transformation.

Victimizers, on the other hand, deny that they are wounded and cover their wounds with a mask of "success" or intimidation. Nevertheless, their behavior is unconsciously wound-driven, and they continue to hurt others in the way that they were hurt in the past. The challenge for those who do not feel their pain is to learn to feel the pain that they are causing to others. In this way they can come to know their own pain.

However, those who have sociopathic or narcissistic tendencies do not learn this very easily. Others may have to push back at them or set clear and firm boundaries with them to get their attention. As long as victims have difficulty saying "No" and standing up for themselves, victimizers will continue to live and act without awareness of their trespasses on others or the pain that they cause.

Of course, when we dominate and control others, we don't usually feel their pain or our own. This rigid denial of our pain makes healing nearly impossible for us.

Neither denying our pain nor identifying with it are strategies for growth and transformation. Yes, we need to feel our pain, and the pain of others, in order to begin the healing journey. But that is just the first step.

The next step is to learn to hold our pain, and the pain of others, compassionately, without identifying with it or being defined by it. This is a lot trickier than it may seem

PAIN VS SUFFERING

Pain and suffering are related but they are not the same thing. Suppose you stub your toe and you have a sudden excruciating pain. You know immediately what the cause of the pain is and you know that if you wait and breathe with the pain for a few moments the pain will go away.

Suffering has a lot to do not just with the pain we feel, but with how we interpret or "hold the pain." When we hold the pain with understanding and compassion, we don't make it worse than it is. We may even make it better. But when we hold the pain with anger, fear, self-judgment or judgment of others, we make the pain worse than it is.

That means that our psychological reaction to the pain has a big impact on the pain we experience and how long it continues. This mind/body connection has been well documented.

Those who live in victim consciousness and shame and blame others for the pain they feel often intensify and/or prolong the pain, perhaps even making it chronic. Those who forgive themselves and others and take responsibility for their own experience often mitigate the pain or shift (transcend) its intensity.

To put it simply: **your thoughts and feelings have a profound effect on what your experience is. How you look at something changes your experience of it.**

So what one person experiences as hardship and attack, another can experience as a challenge and an opportunity to learn. The person who felt attacked makes the attack real and reacts to it by attacking back, shutting down, or running away. So his experience of pain is prolonged.

But the person who refuses to take offense, sees the fear behind the attack and does not react. Her pain is short-lived. It is experienced for an instant and then released.

YOUR FRIEND

Your friend has a story about herself and she lives inside that story. She can tell you all of the reasons why she is not okay and why she needs to be fixed. She can also tell you all the reasons why she will never succeed.

Her story is a self-fulfilling prophecy. She believes that she can't change her life and so she keeps reinforcing the story and living it over and over again.

In order for her to succeed in life she would have to see the story and recognize that it is not true. Then, perhaps, she could change the story.

One simple way of changing the story is to change the first sentence to "I am okay the way I am and there is nothing that needs to be fixed." If she could do that she would stop living as a victim. Instead of saying "I can't" she would say "I can." That too would become a self-fulfilling prophecy.

That seems to be a simple change, does it not? Just changing the story from "I can't" to "I can" moves her from victim consciousness to self empowerment.

The concept is not hard to understand. But the change we are talking about is monumental. Most people are simply not up to it. The reason is that we are attached to our victim consciousness.

We have all been wounded by life and instead of attending to our wounds so that they can be healed, we use them as an excuse for why we can't succeed in life or why we have a right to control and beat up on others.

Both the denial of our wounds and the identification with our wounds are different ways in which we remain stuck in victim consciousness, refusing to heal and take responsibility for our lives.

As long as we continue to live in victim consciousness, as long as we give our power away or usurp the power of others, transformation is not going to be possible for us. We will simply become our story and our pain and suffering will become chronic and predictable.

ENDING THE PROJECTION OF OUR PAIN

Most of the pain and suffering in this world result from the projection of the repressed (unseen) and unredeemed (unintegrated) shadow.

As soon as you stop projecting your pain and start taking responsibility for bringing love to the unloved parts of yourself, something quintessential shifts. Now you are in dialog with your pain. Now you are asking "what is the message here? What is the lesson that needs to be learned?"

Now you are learning to hold the pain compassionately, without blaming others or yourself. You are learning to hold it gently and humbly. As a result, your relationship to your pain begins to shift. Your pain takes you into a deeper communion with yourself.

If pain is really a wake-up call, then once we wake up our pain is no longer needed. When the message has been heard, the messenger can go home.

And the message is always one of love. Love yourself and love your neighbor and all of this will pass. War and hunger will end. Swords will be turned in plowshares.

No, we have not seen that world yet. Martin Luther King said "I may not get there with you, but … we as a people will get to the promised land."

I have no doubt that he was right. Where else can we go? Out of the trenches of hatred, prejudice and injustice, there is only one place to go. We must go from the darkness to the light, from prejudice to acceptance, from injustice to equality.

Without Heaven, Hell has no meaning.

Hell may be a frightening experience for all of us, but it is just a temporary place. It is the place where we descend to know that we must find the light and become it.

PRACTICE, PRACTICE, PRACTICE

In my work I find many people coming to workshops and retreats in a rush to wake up, become enlightened, empowered and ready to share their creative gifts with the world. Even though I tell them they must be very patient if they want to succeed, very few believe me. They push the river and wake up stranded on the river bank. This happens to them over and over again.

The truth is you cannot ride the river until you learn to row and to swim. To try to do so before you are ready is foolish and can even be dangerous.

No matter what path you are on, there is no substitute for spiritual practice. And spiritual practice requires a lot of patience and discipline. It means showing up every day, even when it is hard or inconvenient.

Those who wake up are the ones who want it the most and have learned to be patient. You cannot rush the healing process. It has a rhythm and a timetable of its own.

The river is stronger than you are. Sooner or later, it teaches you to be humble.

As I have pointed out in my book *Healing Your Life*, you cannot step into your power as an awakened human being until you have made substantial progress healing the split in your psyche. Only then is your integration to be trusted and given legs or wings. The gifts you have brought into this life must wait for their full expression until this psychospiritual synergy happens within. That is when the True Self is born. That is when the Phoenix rises from the ashes of the False Self.

Only when your love for yourself is unconditional, when it is deep and wide enough to hold your own fear compassionately, can your suffering diminish substantially and can you step into the fullness of your power and purpose.

SHORTCUTS END IN CUL DE SACS

We all want to find a quicker way to heaven, one that does not ask us to look so deeply at ourselves. But short cuts inevitably end in cul de sacs and delay the journey.

Unfortunately, there are no magic bullets, drugs, mantras or hocus pocus that can take you to psychological wholeness and empowerment. You must go the way all have gone who have taken the journey before you: step by step, moment by moment.

It takes a lifetime to learn to love yourself unconditionally. If you think otherwise, you are just deluding yourself. Better to keep your mask on than to take it off and descend into the shadows before you are really ready.

Those who try to take the rocketship to heaven inevitably crash and burn. Their journey is not one of integration and wholeness, but one of disintegration and fragmentation. That is why it is not surprising that many high-octane spiritual seekers end up going over the edge.

PART ONE

Acceptance
and Responsibility

CHAPTER ONE

Acknowledging Our Pain

When the young Gautama left his father's palace, he was shocked to see human misery. Having been protected all his life and kept safe within the palace walls, he had never witnessed hunger, poverty, disease, cruelty, inequality or injustice. Entering the world beyond the palace was for him a huge awakening.

Now that he saw how others lived, Gautama soon realized that seeking pleasure and avoiding pain could no longer satisfy him and indeed created a disturbing disconnection between himself and the humans who lived outside the palace gates.

So he left the palace and retreated into the forest where he practiced various forms of austerity. Like other spiritual seekers, he sought to bring pain onto himself so that he could learn to transcend it. In time, he found that these practices simply made his soul contract and did not bring him closer to spiritual understanding or intimacy with others.

THE METAPHOR

Like Gautama, all of us, sooner or later, encounter pain. Even if we have been protected by our parents we experience some form of wounding as we journey into the world. Some of us are wounded in utero or in early childhood. Others are wounded later.

Yet no matter what your specific story is, the reality is that suffering—the experience of pain and hardship—is a universal phenomenon.

You can deny your pain, but denial is only a temporary fix. The pain is just pushed inward, where it lurks in the shadows of the psyche. It is only a matter of time before it erupts and when it does it can devastate a life built in denial. In time, like Gautama, we have to encounter our pain and that of others and begin a lifelong journey of healing that takes us through all the highs and lows of our human experience.

WOUNDED HEALERS

Gautama was not a wounded healer. He did not try to heal others before he healed himself. Neither did Jesus or any of the other great spiritual teachers of the world. They started by looking at their own pain. They started by looking at their own consciousness. And you must do the same.

It is not possible to heal our relationships with others before we heal our relationship to self.

The healing of the world around us directly depends on the healing that we experience within our own consciousness.

The story of human suffering—yours and mine—is vividly portrayed in the Old Testament. Job is a favorite son of God. He keeps all of the laws. He does what God wants him to do to the best of his ability. Yet he meets a cruel fate. His family is taken from him. His health is destroyed. He suffers one form of distress after the other.

Yet Job never loses his faith. Somewhere in his heart of hearts he knows that God loves him and wants the best for him. Even though all of the outward signs suggest that God is punishing him and that perhaps he deserves it, Job does not buy in. He knows that he is innocent.

Like our brother Job, we too are innocent. God does not want to punish us or make us suffer. Sometimes, when we look at how we are being attacked by others or how our lives are falling apart, it is hard for us to believe that we are innocent and that God is on our side.

But lest we find our faith and connect with our innocence as Job did, we will become a casualty of life. We will become convinced that we are bad, that we deserve to be punished and we will live in misery as victims.

If you are going to stop living in victim consciousness, here are a few recognitions you must cultivate.

RECOGNITION NUMBER 1

Like Job you must know that you are not bad and you are not unworthy. You may be confused. You may have made a mistake, but your mistakes do not define you, unless you refuse to learn from them. If you have made a mistake, you must take responsibility for it. You must not blame it on anyone else or you will not be able to correct it.

RECOGNITION NUMBER 2

God does not want to punish you. God wants you to understand yourself and others more deeply. God wants you to be a more sensitive and compassionate human being. Some things happen to wake you up and open your heart. That is not a punishment.

Sometimes you may be asked to release an attachment or let go of something you no longer need. That is not a punishment. Shiva, the God of destruction, does not come to punish you but to set you free.

RECOGNITION NUMBER 3

If you believe that God, life or the Universe is punishing you, or if you believe that your pain or suffering is anyone else's responsibility, then you are choosing to live as a victim. Victims give their power away. They do not learn their lessons. They do not forgive themselves or others.

They do not grow. They do not rebound from challenges or adversity. They live in the past. They refuse to let go, die and be reborn.

RECOGNITION NUMBER 4

All this is about you. It is not about anyone else. Your suffering is your responsibility, not anyone else's. When you accept responsibility for the contents of your consciousness, you take back your power. You become able to learn and to grow. You become capable of transforming your relationship to yourself and your world.

CHAPTER TWO

Transforming Our Relationship With Ourselves

Some of us have a good mask. We pretend to be happy. We show up the way others want us to and do our best to meet their needs and our own. We live on the surface of life and rarely touch our pain. It is only when life deals us a major blow that our mask cracks open and we sit face to face with our fears, our judgments, and our unworthiness.

Our shadow self was always there, we just refused to look at it. But now we are forced to look. We are forced to acknowledge the part of ourselves that we cannot accept or love. That is the moment when our spiritual journey begins, when we acknowledge our shadow and begin the long journey from the darkness into the light.

In that moment we get real. We see that we have not learned to love ourselves and how that inability undermines our closest relationships with others. We admit that self-judgment, indeed self-hatred, lurks there at the bottom of our experience, where our heart cries out for love in a world where pain and suffering seem to predominate.

It is in that place where we make the most important choice of our lives: the choice to be a victim swimming in a deep pool of unworthiness and shame, or to learn to be the bringer of love to our own experience. It is here that we decide to close the shades and hide in the shadows or that we learn to find the light and shine it on all the dark places within.

It takes courage to look at our shame and unworthiness. It takes skillfulness to recognize our fear without being overwhelmed or defined by it. And it takes patience with and compassion for the hurt little child in us who has been wounded deeply and doesn't trust anyone.

THE WOUNDED CHILD

The wounded child is a metaphor for your shadow self. Seeing it as a child is important, because it calls you to be a compassionate parent. The child is starved for love, acceptance, and encouragement and these have rarely come from others. Now, you realize that you must be the one who brings the love.

Your job is to love the unlovable parts of yourself that you have repressed or projected onto others. When you project these shadow aspects onto others, they are reflected back to you. People push your buttons and show you the parts of yourself that you have not learned to love.

The attempt to change or fix others is futile. They are just a mirror of you. If you realize that, you won't waste your time in shame or blame. They will only deepen your suffering. Instead, you will learn to look in the mirror and love the one who looks back at you.

Relationships give you one of the greatest tools for waking up. Other people show you where love needs to be brought, not to them, but to the love-starved child within. When the child within feels loved and accepted, he begins to grow up. The gap between you (the spiritual adult) and the wounded child (your shadow) diminishes. Integration and healing begin to happen in the psyche.

The person who drops his or her mask, looks at the shadow and brings love to the unloved parts of self, overcomes the schizophrenic divide, unifying the dualities within. Now high and low, dark and light, male and female, commingle. The work of integration continues and gradually wholeness is born within.

This of course is a conscious journey that we take through the unconscious. The light of awareness descends into the darkness and redeems the wounded children who hide in the shadows. When light comes to the darkness, the darkness is illumined.

The clouds of unconscious self-loathing may return — for this is not a linear journey — but even then there is the remembrance of the light, far away although it may seem. Once the light is acknowledged it cannot be forgotten. It can only be dimmed. That is the key to the faith of one like Job, who held onto the light within, even when the dark clouds gathered around him.

No one likes to feel pain. No one likes to feel sadness. Yet pain and sadness are an inevitable part of our lives. It would be great if we could banish them, but we can't. And any attempt to do so is just pretense. Most of the charlatans disguised as spiritual teachers will promise you heaven and deliver you to hell.

It's not really their fault. You were the one who believed their promises. And you are responsible for what you believe and the path that you follow. Don't be so gullible. Don't give up your power to those who are only too happy to take it and use it to feed their selfishness and their greed.

If you stay with the pain and sadness, instead of trying to avoid it, you will learn something important. Sadness softens you. It opens your heart. It helps you appreciate joy when it comes. And pain tells you what is out of balance. It tells you what is not working in your life so that you can make an adjustment, a shift, and come back into balance. Pain requires healing. And healing is a magnificent process.

If there is no pain, there will be no need for healing. We can all play golf or go walk on the beach. Wouldn't that be nice?

Unfortunately, the only ones who claim to feel no pain are the ones who are in denial. If someone tells you he has already healed, better be skeptical. Some things in life are just too good to be true.

The ones who have healed do not brag about it. They do not advertise their wares for sale in the marketplace. They walk humbly and help when they can. But you will not find them if you seek them. So don't even try.

When you are doing the work they will walk at your side. They come when they know you are ready and not until.

Instead, be with your sadness and your pain. Learn to accept and love yourself. That is your job. Find your faith, like Job did, in the trenches and gullies of life. Spirituality is not about fancy robes and expensive cars. It is not about worldly power. It is about finding the thread of love in a tapestry of pain. It is about finding truth in the desert.

No wonder so few want to walk the path to authentic self-realization.

INNOCENCE ON THE CROSS

Jesus told us to be honest and authentic and to stand for the truth even when we are attacked by others who feel threatened by us. And by doing this himself, he began his painful journey to the cross.

It is not unusual that those who speak from the heart and tell the truth to power are ostracized or persecuted. That is the way of the world. Those who live in denial cannot bear the truth, for the truth would condemn their way of life and call them to a higher path.

Denial may have its price, but they will avoid paying that price as long as they can.

They are the ones who lift Jesus onto the cross, the ones who cram the Jews into the trains heading to the ovens, the ones who are afraid to stand up to power and instead become the instruments of crucifixion and geno-cide. All of human history illustrates this.

There is no country, no race, no religion where this story has not been written and told again and again.

The Bible tells us that Jesus died for our sins, but how can that be? Jesus did not die even for his own sins, much less for ours. He died because he was innocent and unafraid and condemned by powerful people living in fear. They used their worldly power in the attempt to squash the truth. But, as we know, they did not succeed. In fact, they made the truth shine like a beacon all over the earth.

You can kill people, but you cannot kill the truth. One man died on the cross, but the truth that he spoke lives forever in the hearts of the people.

So what about the suffering of Jesus? Did Jesus feel pain when he was crucified? I know people who insist that he did not, but what if he did? Did suffering make him less Godly? If God is to become human, isn't he bound to experience suffering?

The crucifixion of Jesus symbolizes the pain that the heart feels when it is violated and misunderstood. It reflects the suffering of all people who have been forsaken and abused. It demonstrates that no person, not even Jesus, goes through this life unwounded.

The good news is not that Jesus did not suffer. The good news is that Jesus was healed, made whole and restored to his rightful place. As it was for him, so it will be for us.

As the Rabbi says "bad things happen to good people." Job knew that all too well. Perhaps you know it as well.

None of us can control what happens in this life. Each one of us is given something difficult to chew on his plate. That is not because we are bad or unworthy. Jesus was not bad or unworthy, yet look what he was asked to bear!

Whatever our experience is we must learn to show up for it. Bitching and moaning, complaining, blaming and shaming do not help us show up. In fact, they make showing up impossible.

Life may stun us and throw us off course. It may wound us or beat us down. It may undermine the ground under our feet. But as long as we can stand up, we must do so. We must fight the good fight. We must cling to our innocence and self-worth. We must remember again and again that we deserve acceptance and love, no matter what our life looks like.

While the world would look at us uncharitably and find fault with us, we cannot allow ourselves to be defined from the outside. We must see and define ourselves from the inside out. Others may not understand us or see us clearly. They may impose their judgments and expectations. They may say that we have failed. But very likely none of this is true.

People "see through a glass darkly." They see through the filter of their fear, their shame, and their judgments. They do not see us face to face. They do not see who we really are. And we don't see them either.

Only when we see from the heart, only when we see with the eyes of love, do we see who we really are and who others truly are. We must realize that in each moment we have the choice to see through the eyes of fear or to see through the eyes of love.

And we must start with ourselves. We must ask "Am I loving myself right now? Am I being gentle with myself or am I judging myself? Am I blessing or am I condemning?" How we see ourselves and how we see others are two sides of the same coin. We cannot really love another and hate ourselves, nor can we hate another and love ourselves.

Love is not something conditional that can be manipulated and given to some and withheld from others. Love is all inclusive. It starts in your heart and extends to everyone. If it is not limitless, then it is not love. It is something else.

That something else has ruled the world for thousands of years. It is behind all the collective heartache and betrayal. It is the ego structure that seeks our survival at any cost and even masquerades in the name of morality and religion.

The truth is the ego cannot heal itself. It cannot take one through the minefield of fear to the threshold of love. It keeps tripping itself up. And every time it trips, thousands are maimed and mutilated.

We don't know what a world illumined by love would look like. Here and there perhaps we have seen signs, but they are few and far between. Suffice it to say that such a world will not be given to us by others, not even by Jesus.

We are the bringers of love to our own experience.

When we learn to love ourselves radically and consistently, we will be a messenger of love in this world, calling others to the truth within their own hearts.

Each soul wrestles with the angel until the angel yields. And S/he will not yield until the power of love demands it.

CHAPTER THREE

Cultivating Love

It seems that "love" is a very difficult word for us. When I tell people their number one responsibility is to learn to love themselves, they often look at me with a blank stare. "But how do we do that?" they ask, again and again.

"This is not some esoteric task," I tell them. "It is an ordinary one."

You love yourself by being nice to yourself. You know how to be kind to others so just turn that around and be nice to yourself. You know how to be gentle and patient with others so turn it around and be gentle and patient with yourself. You know how to stop judging others and accept them as they are, so stop judging yourself and accept yourself as you are.

You know how to stop yelling at others. You know how to speak in a loving way toward them. So stop yelling at yourself and start talking to yourself using the language of love. Say "I am a good person. I am doing the best that I can. I deserve my love and respect."

When you notice that you are being harsh and impatient

with yourself, say "I need to give myself a break, stop pushing myself, stop putting pressure on myself, stop judging myself…. Let me take a breath and come back into my heart. Let me remember that I am okay the way I am right now. I am not broken and I don't need to be fixed."

Of course, cultivating love is a spiritual practice. You don't master it right away. You have spent most of your life cultivating self-judgment and feeling unworthy (albeit unconsciously), so you aren't going to reverse these habits overnight.

This practice asks you to *become conscious* or *aware* of all the times when you are mean to yourself or start to beat yourself up. In the past you have done this unconsciously and it led to all kinds of self-sabotage. But now you want to be aware of it. You need to recognize it. You need to catch it. Say to yourself, "Wow! I am really being hard on myself right now. Let me soften a little. Let me take a breath." That's all.

Don't make yourself bad or wrong for being hard on yourself or you will be using your spiritual practice to beat yourself up. Be careful. The ego is very tricky. It is always finding fault with you or somebody else.

Just be aware of what's happening with compassion for yourself. You don't have to change anything. Awareness itself is all that is necessary.

In time, awareness begins to do its work. All that was unconscious — all those hidden beliefs and reactive patterns — become conscious and come up for healing. And healing happens organically, without asking much from you. As soon as you see the ways in which you are not loving yourself, you naturally turn away from them. When the blocks to love are seen, they move aside and all that remains is love.

When all the ways in which you feel shame and judge

yourself are brought into compassionate awareness, you naturally release them. You know that is not who you are. You stop seeing the world through the lens of fear and you no longer see a guilty world.

The world you see through the eyes of love is a world purified and transformed. That is why Jesus told us "First take the beam out of your own eye, and then you will see clearly."

How we behold the world determines the world that we see. And we cannot help but behold the world through the lens of our own consciousness and experience.

Unconscious fear and shame distort our perception and create a great drama in which there are endless victims and victimizers. That drama, along with the suffering that accompanies it, will continue until we learn to make our own fear and shame conscious.

We can start in a simple way by looking carefully at how we speak and act toward ourselves. "Am I speaking to myself in a loving way or am I yelling at myself, pressuring myself and putting myself down?" If I am addressing myself in an unkind way, let me be aware of it and see if I can be more gentle with myself in this moment.

This is a simple practice, the profundity of which you will not recognize until you have made it an integral part of your conscious experience.

TWO SIDES OF THE SAME COIN

If you do not love yourself, how can you love your brother and sister? Learning to love yourself is job number one.

Yet if you do not love your brother and sister, how can you love yourself? Learning to love others is job number two.

These are two sides of the same coin. Sometimes it comes up heads and sometimes it comes us tails. If you make progress with one side, the other side becomes easier.

Now just change the words a bit.

If you do not forgive yourself, how can you forgive your brother and sister? Yet if you do not forgive your brother and sister, how can you forgive yourself?

Jesus tells us "As we give so shall we receive." That is one of the spiritual laws of life.

So, at the same time that you are cultivating a loving relationship with yourself, you can cultivate a loving relationship with others. Using both practices simultaneously makes them more powerful and effective.

If you judge others, don't blurt out your judgments. Instead, be aware of your judgments. Recognize that they have to do with your own unconscious fear and shame and have very little to do with the person you are judging. You simply project your fear and shame onto others because you are afraid to look at them directly.

In all interactions with others, ask yourself, "Is there something helpful I can do or say?" If not, refrain from speaking or acting.

Say and do whatever you can to encourage others, appreciate them and cheer them up, but don't try to fix them or be their savior.

All attempts to fix or redeem others are simply attack in disguise and demonstrate your own need for healing.

Practice good boundaries and allow others the space to take responsibility for their own lives and solve their own problems. Otherwise you will interfere inappropriately in their lives and create a big mess for them and for yourself.

Being kind to others does not mean agreeing to do something you don't feel comfortable doing just because you are asked to do it. It does not mean sacrifice.

What you give to others must be given freely, without expectation of getting something in return. You give because you are able to do so and it is a pleasure to give.

Giving is a dynamic act that creates a natural energy exchange. The energy we put out to help others eventually comes back to us, not directly perhaps, but in unanticipated and surprising ways. When we give, we enter the dance of life happily, not knowing where it will take us, but trusting the energy that moves us.

True abundance comes when we move in the flow of life and naturally share our wisdom, our resources and our creative gifts. Because we trust the current of life, the river keeps flowing from one heart and mind to another. When resistances arise, we release them to the current and they take us safely through our fear to places we have not yet known.

When you have more than you need, the natural thing is to share it with others. When you try to hold onto your resources, you create a dam in the river and the energy builds up. Eventually the dam is compromised and all that you tried to withhold and protect flies down the river. Better to let the river come and go at will. It is wiser than you are.

In the story of the fishes, one fish multiplies so that the multitude can be fed. Jesus has a deep and abiding faith that whatever we have is enough. Lack is not possible, for the river is abundant and if our hearts and minds are open, all of our needs can be met.

Can we live in this consciousness, being grateful for what we have and knowing that it is enough? Can we feed not only ourselves but all around us who need to be fed, loved, and nurtured? Jesus never turned any one away. Can that be said about you or me?

The depth of heart of the one who was baptized in these waters cannot be fathomed. It is beyond the capacity of the mind to imagine. But he who submits to the river lives in a state of trust with the universe. The power of the river moves him and moves through him to us. That is how wondrous things come to be when we least expect them.

Do not forget, he invited us into the stream. He invited us to love and to trust the river. And he told us that what he could do, we could do and more.

My friends Stephen and Barbara wrote a song that says:

"There is a river of love flowing through our hearts,
from me to you, and a river of love
flowing through our hearts, from you to me,
and all I feel is this river of love, flowing in harmony,
and all I feel is this river of love, flowing eternally."

Like Buddha, Jesus knew the power of the river and he knew that it flows through each one of us in its journey to the sea.

CHAPTER FOUR

Ending the Patterns of Self-Betrayal

Most of us have lived for many years in self-betrayal, trying to show up the way others want us to. We may choose the career or the spouse mom or dad wanted us to choose, only to find out that we have made a big mistake. In the attempt to please others and win their love and acceptance, we betray ourselves. We ignore the strengths and gifts we were born with. We try to become someone we are not.

Self-betrayal inevitably leads to suffering.

Yet we cannot beat ourselves up for this. We all do it. We do not come into this life knowing who we are, so we try to become the person we think we are supposed to become. Inevitably, we find it does not work. So then we begin to ask the questions "Who am I and what do I really want? What are my greatest gifts? What brings me the greatest joy and enables me to share that joy with others?"

It may take us a while to answer these questions. But the questions become a tool for discovering who we really are.

Self-betrayal, as unpleasant as it is, is part of the process of our overall growth and transformation. We have to know who we are not, in order to begin to figure out who we are. The False Self must be created and destroyed for the True Self to be born.

The round peg does not fit into the square hole. The attempt to force the peg into the hole is uncomfortable, if not painful. And it is always futile. If you are an artist at heart you aren't going to be happy being an attorney, even though mommy and daddy and your favorites teachers thought it would be a good idea. If you are gay, you aren't going to be happy in a heterosexual relationship even if it gives you the status and normalcy you want.

Sooner or later you will have to stop the self-betrayal and build yourself an art studio or come out of the closet with your friends and family. Sooner or later, you will have to honor who you are and ask others to accept you. And, if they don't accept you, you will have to have the courage to live your truth in the face of rejection or ostracism.

For most of us self-betrayal comes to a head when we go through our mid-life crisis. For some it happens earlier.

Whenever it happens, it can seem like our lives are falling apart. Humpty Dumpty comes off the wall and smashes into thousands of pieces. Others may think that we are having a nervous breakdown. But in truth we are going into Spiritual Crisis. We are entering a time when old definitions of self, old roles and responsibilities no longer work and a new vision of self must be born.

This is a time of spiritual rebirth. The labor pains may be intense, but they are part of a process that will transform our lives for the better.

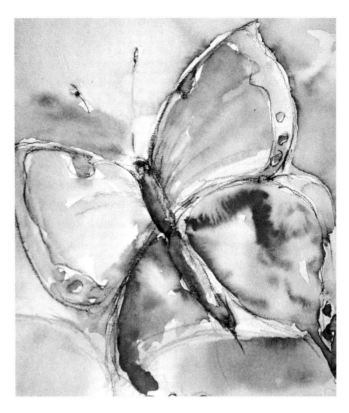

Like the caterpillar we emerge from the cocoon with brightly colored wings. We no longer need to walk along the ground laboring in sacrifice, doing a job we hate, staying in a loveless relationship, living in a state of depression with little faith in ourselves or our future.

As we go through our spiritual crisis, we free ourselves from a past that has become dysfunctional and is holding us back. And we enter our new life like a child, innocent, playful and eyes wide open.

Of course that doesn't mean that life all of a sudden becomes easy for us. We have a lot to learn to be successful in our new life. And we need to step up to the challenges before us. But now we are motivated from within to take the next step. We know that we are moving forward at our own pace with the gifts we have been given. Now we are living with integrity, congruence, meaning and purpose.

Something important has changed. We are learning to honor ourselves.

BREAKING OUT OF PRISON

We all compare ourselves to others because we want to fit in and gain social acceptance and approval. We want our friends, our family and our community to think well of us. We conform to family expectations and social norms because it seems the right thing to do and we believe it will make us happy.

Unfortunately, conformity shuts down our soul's need to grow and individuate. We aren't here to be like others. We are here to learn to be ourselves. Of course, that is not an easy task, but it is a necessary one and we will not be happy until we accomplish it.

You can have all the power and riches in the world. People can appreciate you and look up to you. But none of this satisfies if you know this is not who you really are. In the end, you will give all of this up, just to have a chance to know and to be yourself.

That is the good news. The bad news is that you can waste the majority of your life living out a drama that you disdain.

But it is never too late to throw the masks and disguises away and let people know the truth about you. Sure, it is scary. You became this False Self because you were afraid that people would reject you if you showed your uniqueness. And those fears still lurk within. If you want to be free and authentic, you must face your fear of rejection. You must be willing to take the chance that others will turn away from you when you tell the truth about yourself.

They are attached to the old you. The new you may terrify them.

That's just the way it is. It is their problem, not yours, and you cannot keep yourself in prison just to appease their fear or your own. Or you can. It is your choice. You have the key to the prison door.

Nobody else is going to force you to grow or to change. But if you stay in prison too long, your soul may become restless. And no prison or prisoner is a match for a restless soul.

THE PHOENIX RISES

This is the setup. We build up the False Self to acquire the love and approval of others.

This does not work. Our heart is not in it. So we go into crisis and in time the False Self just falls apart. We can't sustain it anymore. Out of the ashes of the False Self, the Phoenix rises. The True Self is born.

All the angels in heaven are applauding. For another soul is standing up to shine its light.

Meanwhile, your spouse, your children, your friends, your co-workers may be aghast. They may think you have lost your mind. They want you to remain the person you used to be. They like the old you.

You may try for a while to appease them. But the longer you stay, the more restless your soul becomes. If you wait too long, your soul will summon up the wind and a great storm will come and destroy the prison walls so that you have no choice but to leave.

Some change comes out of the blue. It is sudden, unanticipated, and irrevocable. We can complain all we want, but it won't do us any good.

Job knew that. He knew in the end he had to submit to God's will.

Changes that are needed for the soul to grow may be made voluntarily. There will be challenges and growing pains as we learn to transform a life led in self-betrayal into a life that enables us to be honest and authentic. Voluntary change — cooperating with our soul's need to grow — can be made without collateral damage. But involuntary change — change that comes after we have repeatedly refused to answer our soul's wake up calls — can shake our lives to their foundation.

Only you know whether or not you have been procrastinating and ignoring your soul's call for transformation. If you have, you might want to move everything else to the back burner and focus on making immediate changes in your life that end your self-betrayal.

We all want to fit in, but the truth is that each one of us is on a unique journey. Sooner or later we must learn to embrace our own truth and have the courage to live it in this life. That is what our soul wants. If we oppose that inner force that seeks individuation, it will literally explode the form that holds it back. Better to cooperate now while we have the conscious choice.

CHAPTER FIVE

Setting Healthy Boundaries

Of course, it will be more difficult for us to honor ourselves if we betray others or interfere inappropriately in their lives. We must learn to give to others the freedom that we claim for ourselves.

If I do not allow you to be you, how can I ask you to allow me to be me?

Like all spiritual ideas, this one works both ways.

To ensure my own need to individuate I must support and defend your right to be your authentic self. Since you are different from me in your gifts, your experience, your values, I may be forced to stretch to support you. If you come from a different race, religion, gender or sexual orientation, it may be hard for me to accept you as you are and support your right to be yourself and to have complete equality in this world. But I must learn to support you and to fight for your right to be you. If I don't, I may undermine my own freedom.

To fight for freedom and equality requires a good understanding of boundaries. I don't have to like you or want to be like you to support your freedom and your equality with me. You don't have to like me or want to be like me either.

Your life belongs to you and you are responsible for it. It is not for me to judge you or dictate to you. As long as you respect me and give me the space to be me, I can and must do the same for you.

Unfortunately, we are all very threatened by differences. If I am straight and you are gay, and I see that more and more people are coming out as gay, I may feel that my own sexual preferences are being threatened. Of course that isn't true, but that may be my knee-jerk reaction. And if it is, then that means I don't have a good understanding of boundaries.

The truth is that I may be the only straight person left in the world, but as long as you respect and support me as an individual, I don't have to feel threatened.

Our good and that of our brother and sister is one and the same. It does not matter which group is in the majority. It is the duty and responsibility of all majorities to respect and safeguard the rights of minority groups.

One of the erroneous beliefs people have is that love is based on agreement. If I agree with you, then I love you and vice versa. But it is not true. **Love is not based on agreement. Love is based on acceptance**. And acceptance of differences is the key to creating a world of equality in which we all honor and respect each other.

A CRASH COURSE IN BOUNDARIES

I have worked with many people over the years and trespass is an issue for all of us.

It seems difficult for us to understand where our right and responsibility begins and ends and where the right and responsibility of another person begins. As a result, we inevitably move into projection. That is when the insanity starts and misunderstandings and wounds result.

To help all of us take responsibility for own stuff and take others off the hook, I came up with the crash course in boundaries. Here it is in one sentence:

Everything I think, feel, say, and do belongs to me, and everything you think, feel, say and do belongs to you.

If you use this simple truth in your daily life, you will stay out of needless conflicts and find a way to honor yourself and others.

You will claim your freedom to have your own experience and to learn to be responsible for it. And you will give others the same opportunity to be themselves and to take responsibility for the choices they make.

CHOOSE YOUR FRIENDS WISELY

Whenever we are wrapped in victim consciousness, we are not able to give love to ourselves or to others.

If you surround yourself with people who are living in victim consciousness, it won't be easy for you to connect with love. If you are wise, you will set boundaries with people who are constantly shaming and blaming and recirculating negative thoughts. Send them love, but keep them at a safe distance.

It is impossible to pull someone else out of the muck without getting pulled in. So don't try. You are not their savior. And when they want to come out they will.

If you or anyone else is stuck in a rut, you can dig it deeper or climb out.

You can feel sorry for yourself or feel grateful for the gifts you still have. That's the choice.

In each moment you can identify with your fears and those of others, or you can connect to the love within your heart and share it with others.

Love is both a state of consciousness and a way of life. A life lived in love is completely different than a life lived in fear. But you cannot live a life in love, if you do not cultivate love within your heart. That is the birthing chamber

CHAPTER SIX

Claiming Our Inner Authority

Jesus told us to give to Caesar what is due to him and to give to God what is due to God.

We can be a good citizen of the world and obey the laws that help us to live peacefully and in harmony. We can stop at the red lights and slow down at the yellow ones, although even that is challenging for some of us.

We can do our part to care for our environment and our fellow citizens. But we cannot and should not betray ourselves just to win the approval of others.

There is a whole area of life that does not belong to the collective. That is our spiritual life. Often we ignore our spiritual needs in order to make money, find a spouse, and have a family. There is nothing wrong with meeting our survival needs or those of our family. But we have other needs that must be met. We have the need to be ourselves, speak our truth and enter into work and relationships that support our individuation. Those needs are important too and must not be forgotten.

So long as we find a balance between being "in" the world and not "of" the world, we can live a balanced, grounded and spiritual life.

Caesar can tell us to pay our dues and stop at red lights, but Caesar cannot tell us what to believe. He cannot tell us who we are. That is the realm of internal authority.

In life we have to deal with external authority and play by the rules so long as it does not compromise or usurp our inner authority. But each of us must also be free to listen to our heart and to make up our mind.

That is our God-given right and responsibility.

When human laws and institutions (external authority) respect and safeguard our internal authority, we have the freedom to speak and to worship as we want. There is a healthy tension in the body politic. Ideas can be debated and discussed. Divergent voices can be heard. But when human laws and institutions no longer respect and safeguard our inner authority, the conditions become ripe for political revolution.

If we are going to live in a safe, peaceful world that guarantees our freedom, we have to balance the requirements of both internal and external authority. The question for each human being is "how I can listen to my inner guidance and follow my bliss without jeopardizing the safety and security of my family and my community?"

Some people emphasize safety and security at the expense of their personal growth. Others emphasize personal growth and neglect their needs for safety and security.

Neither of these approaches is likely to succeed.

So we are back to God and to Caesar again. We must learn to care both for our inner life and our outer life. We need to find a balance between meeting our worldly needs and meeting our spiritual needs. We need to learn to be in the world without being of the world. We need to listen to our soul's needs without abandoning our inner child or our families.

Granted, this is not an easy business and all of us have made mistakes along the way. Beating ourselves for those mistakes is not going to make it any easier for us to find the balance that we need. Wherever we have erred, let us recognize it and correct it, without overcompensating and going to the other extreme.

PART TWO

Compassionate
Awareness

CHAPTER SEVEN

Denial and Identification

In Part One, we made it clear that the two major obstacles to healing and empowerment are the denial of our pain and the identification with it. Denial prevents us from feeling our pain and that of others. Identification keeps us stuck in our pain and victim consciousness.

Let us look at each pattern just a bit.

First, if you are in denial, it isn't easy for you to feel your pain or that of others. You cover it over with work and responsibilities. Or perhaps you numb it out by using alcohol or drugs.

At one extreme is the narcissist who is preoccupied with his own self-gratification, using others for his own ends. At the other extreme is the caretaker who ignores his own needs and is preoccupied with caring for others.

Neither one is in touch with his feelings. When fear or shame come up, he represses them or projects them onto others. So he never comes to know the hurt, vulnerable child within.

Your major challenge is going to be to get in touch with your pain and meet the child within who feels afraid and unworthy. Inner child work and other forms of emotional healing can help you to do this.

In addition, you are going to have to learn to feel the pain of others. Sometimes it may be easier for you to feel their pain than it is for you to feel your own. That's okay. Walk through either door and you come to the other one.

On the other hand, if you are identified with your pain and wearing it as a badge of honor, seeking sympathy from others, you need to understand that you are simply reinforcing your victim consciousness and powerlessness. You are digging a deeper hole for yourself, and the deeper the hole the more time and energy it will take to climb out of it.

Your greatest challenge is to stop blaming others and making excuses for why you can't succeed and begin to take responsibility for creating the kind of life that you want. You aren't powerless, although you may think and act like you are. You need to stop living small and take back the power you too readily give to others.

Your modus operandi is "I can't do it." And you keep looking for a savior who will do it for you. Better wake up and realize that anyone who volunteers for that role is as wounded as you are. Victims inevitably attract victimizers because they don't believe they can take care of themselves.

This is a game that can go on a very long time. You need to see the pattern and end it. Learn to say "No" to those who would make decisions for you and understand that your life is your responsibility. If you refuse to take responsibility, you give up your power. It is that simple.

Denying our pain or identifying with it are both strategies of self-betrayal. They keep us locked into our dysfunctional patterns and reinforce our suffering.

CULTIVATING COMPASSIONATE AWARENESS

The most important step in our healing process is to be aware of our patterns of self-betrayal. This is profoundly important, yet I find that very few people get it. When you say "be aware" people say "Yes, of course, no problem," as if they were already doing it. But obviously that is not the case.

In order to be aware of something, you must see without resisting it or identifying with it. If you resist or identify with something, you can't be aware of it. You are judging it instead and seeing it through your filters, positive or negative. You are attaching to it or pushing it away.

It is not so easy a task to see without resistance or attachment. It takes a lot of practice.

The only way that you can do it is to bring your awareness not just to what you are looking at, but also to the way in which you are seeing it. So if you judge positively or negatively, you bring awareness to your judgment.

Then you see the judgment without judging it. See "I judge so and so" without making the judgment real or making yourself bad for having it.

Just see it neutrally. That is what it means to hold it compassionately.

When you are compassionately aware of your judgment, you can see that person and yourself clearly. "Here is this person I am judging," you realize, "and I am also judging myself for judging him. But all of this is just a projection of my own shadow. I feel bad, wrong, and unworthy, so I see him that way, and then I feel guilty for doing it."

And then you realize "I don't have to do that anymore. I can be aware of my shame, and stop judging him and blaming myself."

These are the psychological steps involved in seeing your judgments with compassion. You are seeing what your ego is making and then unmaking it. You are removing the blinders through which you see yourself and the world around you.

This sounds complicated, but it really isn't. However, it requires a great deal of practice to do it skillfully. You have to slow down the judgment train to see who is driving it.

Most of us are trying very hard not to have judgments. So when we have judgments, we push them away or sweep them under the carpet. We don't want to look at them. Often, we pretend to be judgment free when we are not.

But if we can have the courage to witness our judgments, we can move through them to the other side. When I acknowledge that I am judging you I begin to see you as you are.

RIDING THE HORSE

Let me give you a silly example. Let us say that seeing your judgments compassionately is like taking care of a horse that is going to take you to a wonderful distant town you want to visit. If you beat that horse, he is not going to make it even to the next town. You have to feed him, give him water, brush him and encourage him, so that he wants to make the journey with you.

Even though you would like to, you aren't going to get rid of your judgments. You aren't going to get rid of your fear and your shame. They are your companions. Hold them gently and they will not get in your way. But judge them harshly and they will undermine everything that you try to do.

In order to ride the horse, you have to be firm but nice to him. Let him know that you are in charge, but let him also see that you are patient and kind. Then, he will relax and accept your guidance when you take the reins.

We all have judgments and yes they do distort our perception of what is.

If you don't see your judgments, you will be living in denial. That is like a horse without a rider. He might get to the promised land, but you won't get there with him.

On the other hand, if you identify with your judgments you make them real. You color the world with your shame and your fear. That is like Richard III without a horse. He has to lie on the battlefield and stew in his own juices.

We have to see what does not work and stop doing it. We need to stop pretending that we don't have judgments. And we need to see those judgments and hold them compassionately. In that way we can thread the needle and stop looking for it in the haystack.

Since awareness is possible for all of us, we have one of the key tools that we need to wake up. We just have to use the tool. We have to commit to our spiritual practice.

Light is another word for awareness. When we are aware of something we shed light on it.

By bringing the light to the shadowy world within, we illumine it. By looking at our judgments, and the wounds and reactive patterns behind them, we begin to see through the various veils and blocks to love within our consciousness.

What we become aware of, or bring the light to, can no longer operate unconsciously. That is the power of awareness. We bring light to the shadowy world within.

The Taoists call this practice "turning around the light." When we shine the light on our inner world, we begin to transform it. Gradually the shadows are illuminated and we see through the veils to Our Core Self.

This is our shining essence, our original innocence.

As long as we keep bringing the light, it happens by itself. We don't have to make it happen.

When you are aware of a judgment, you no longer make it real. It can no longer color your perception. When you are aware of your wound, you stop attracting people who want to wound you and you stop wounding others. For most of us, the cycle of abuse continues only because it operates unconsciously. When we make it conscious, we begin to neutralize its power.

It is not that we make our judgments go away. By seeing them without identifying with them or pushing them away, we disconnect the trigger. The bomb may still be there, but there is no way to explode it. And that gives us time to call the bomb squad in to disassemble the bomb.

For those who commit to inner child healing, the bomb can be taken apart. The cycle of abuse can be consciously ended.

For those who are not drawn to inner child healing work, but who practice compassionate awareness of their judgments, the trigger is detached so that the bomb can no longer explode, causing havoc for themselves and others. Hopefully, your spiritual practice includes one or both of these tools.

NOT FIXING

Of course, there is no quick fix offered here. Indeed, since you are not broken, you don't need to be fixed, nor does anyone else.

Your innocence lies beneath the cloak of your guilt. Take that cloak off and your original innocence survives intact.

We all believe the lies we are told. But once we stop believing them, truth meets us face to face.

Spiritual practice is not about getting something we don't have. It is about removing what is not true so that truth can be seen.

If there were no truth, if there were no innocence, then we would all be doomed to a life in hell. But, as I have said before, hell without heaven makes no sense.

Hell presupposes heaven. Falseness presupposes Truth.

The truth about you is that you are innocent and worthy of love. The same is true about others. If you believe otherwise, you will create a guilty world in which everyone feels unworthy.

Yes, it is true. You have the power to do that. You can take heaven and make it into hell. But if you do that you will have to live in the hell that you made. And guess what? In that world people suffer greatly and their suffering seems to be without end.

If you want to end your suffering, you must realize that you created a guilty world and understand that you have both the power and the responsibility to undo that world. This is not something that happens externally. It happens within your own consciousness.

Your job is to undo what you have made. If you did not make it, you would not be able to undo it. The good news is that you did make it.

God did not make hell on earth. You did.

God made heaven and gave it to you for safe keeping. Like Adam and Eve, you became terrified by the power that was given to you. You were afraid of making mistakes, which of course you did. And then you were afraid that God would punish you.

Guess what? God does not punish you. You punish yourself. You punish your brother and sister. This world of blame and shame, attack and counter-attack was not made by God or with his blessing. This is your creation.

This is the world you created out of shame and fear. And now you must suffer the world that you made until you come face to face with your shame and your fear.

Make them bad, identify with them or deny them, and you will create hell all over again.

But hold them with compassion and learn to be the bringer of love to your own experience and the world made by shame and fear will begin to fade away.

It is, after all, just an illusion.

And then you will realize the power that you have to leave the Garden or to return to it, the prodigal daughter or son.

God did not kick you out of Heaven. You decided to leave. Fortunately, you have a memory of the place of your origin. Perhaps it is in your DNA, or in your heart of hearts. Either way, it will only be a matter of time before you come back to it.

HANSEL AND GRETEL

If you don't like references to the Bible, consider the story of Hansel and Gretel. Their stepmother forced their father to abandon them in the forest (mommy and daddy wound). The first time this happened they found their way back home, but the second time the birds ate the crumbs of bread they had left along the path to guide them back home. So they really were lost and disoriented.

Unprotected in the forest, they were soon preyed upon by an old witch (mommy wound again) who had a house made of sweets. They could not resist the sweets (Some things are too good to be true) and began to eat pieces of the house. Of course, that is what the witch hoped they would do and soon they were prisoners in the witch's house.

The witch made it clear that she intended to fatten them up and eat them. First she would eat Hansel who was locked in a cage and then she would eat Gretel. But Gretel was too smart for the witch. When the day came for Hansel to be cooked in the oven, Gretel asked the witch to test the oven to see if it was hot enough and when the witch bent over to look, Gretel shoved her in.

Hansel and Gretel were innocent but, like us, they were

also wounded. Like it or not, they had to experience the shadowy world of the forest, where they were seduced by the witch, betrayed themselves and gave their power away.

Of course, they were very scared, but they had to hold their fear gently and keep their wits. They had to be aware of the witch's habits and weaknesses in order to take their power back and save their lives. Fortunately, they stayed alert, and vanquished the witch and returned home to their father who was overjoyed to see them.

And what about the wicked stepmother who had convinced their father to abandon them? Well, like the witch, she too had died while the children were in the forest. So now having faced their fears and stood up to their abusers, Hansel and Gretel could live happily.

Of course, they still needed to work out their father wound (the father was an enabler who did not protect them from the stepmother), but that I suppose is another chapter of the story.

GUILT: AN UNCONSCIOUS CREATOR

I know it is a bit of a leap to say that Hansel and Gretel created this drama so that they could wake up. But how else can you explain it?

If they were not powerful, how could they defeat the witch? Of course, once they entered the forest, they became estranged from their innocence and the source of their power. They had to face their fears and rediscover their power.

All victims have the same journey. They betray themselves and give their power away and they have to learn to believe in themselves and take their power back. Of course, that isn't as easy as the fairy tale would suggest. There are many days when they despair and live in terror of the day when the witch will eat them.

We all have fears that must be faced. As we sink into victim consciousness, we feel powerless and lose our confidence and our hope.

That is part and parcel of the drama of sin and redemption. When the light dims around us, we must descend into the darkness to find the light within.

Of course, we feel guilty for the mistakes that we make and we are afraid that we will be punished. That is why we leave home and enter the forest. Our guilt and shame are the architects and builders of this place of suffering where our fears become real and materialize before us as witches, demons and various personifications of evil.

In this place, we punish ourselves and each other. That continues until we remember that we were the ones who made this place and we have the power to un-make it.

We must come to realize that sin itself does not condemn us. We are all sinners. We all make mistakes. We all give our power away. That is just the first half of the story. In part two of the story, we learn from our mistakes, re-affirm our innocence, and take back our power to create our lives.

The question is not "Did we create this vale of tears?" The question is "When will we remember that we did?"

Being an unconscious creator does not help us wake up. We must become conscious of our creations and learn to take responsibility for them. That is when we move out of victimhood and reclaim our power.

CHAPTER EIGHT

Finding the Source

You can't give what you don't have. If you have $100 in your pocket and a beggar approaches you on the street and asks you for money, you might give him $5 or $10. You can even give him all $100. But if your pocket is empty, then you have nothing to give to him.

If you are lonely and needy and you have not learned to love yourself, you can ask your boyfriend to love you, but he probably won't be up to the task. Why is that? Because you always attract a partner who reflects back to you, not what you need, but what you have.

If you don't love yourself, you will attract a partner who does not love himself, and he will be as impotent to love you as you are to love him.

Neediness does not attract abundance. Lack of love does not attract love.

You cannot manifest in the external world something that does not already exist within consciousness. That is true for self-worth (money) and it is true for love.

So if you are poor and hungry for love and approval does that mean there is no hope for you? No, but it does mean that you are bound to fail if you look outside of yourself for salvation. That never works. You won't find a savior who will offer you something you have not learned to give to yourself.

The best you can do is attract a wolf wearing sheep's clothing. So it might be wise to stop looking for a better sheep.

Learn to give to yourself what you would get from others. Love yourself without conditions, be patient and kind to yourself and in time you will attract a partner who will do the same. Get a job. Go to school and learn a marketable skill. Work hard and with a cheerful disposition and you will attract abundance in your life.

What you have achieved within yourself (by and for yourself) you can offer to others. But you cannot give others a benefit you have not earned.

You cannot create out of lack. You can create only out of abundance. You can multiply only what you have. That is a universal law.

So if you feel unworthy and focus on what you don't have, you will just multiply your experience of lack and unworthiness. After a while, this becomes a bit discouraging and you have to admit it just isn't going to work.

In order to change the outside, you have to change the inside. Fortunately for you and for all of us, no one is really empty of love or worthiness. However, the belief that you are not worthy of love can be a self-fulfilling prophecy.

So you need to challenge that belief whenever it arises in consciousness. Every time you feel powerless or sorry for yourself, you need to see that you are reinforcing a belief that needs to be corrected.

The source of love and abundance is within you, not outside you. To connect to the Source and feel the love energy of the universe you must be willing to open yourself to it. And to open yourself, you need to let go of your negative thinking. You have to stop being run by your fears.

Hold your fears gently and look at all the ways in which you find fault with yourself, but have compassion for the hurt little kid within you. Learn to be the good daddy or mommy who brings love to the wounded child. Be the bringer of love, for that is what you are.

If love was not your essence, then no transformation would be possible. But because love is your essence, you can find the source and draw from it. You can become the bringer of love to your own experience.

When you bring love to yourself you have love to give. The more love you bring to yourself and give to others without expectation of return, the more you deepen the supply of love that is available to you.

THE BUCKET BRIGADE

Think of it this way. You have been given a bucket, but you don't know why. The riverbed is dry. The ground is parched and nothing of value grows. But under the floor of your house is a spring. Sometimes you can hear it at night.

One day some water comes out of the ground and you get your bucket and fill it up. You carry that water into your village and offer it to your neighbors. They are so grateful they offer you gifts in return.

Then you say to them "If this spring was under my

house, maybe it is under your house too." So everyone gets a shovel and a bucket and finds her own supply.

Now there is enough water to supply the whole village and to irrigate the fields so that crops can grow again.

Now there is abundance. But where did that abundance come from? It came from being present in your life and finding the source.

That is what each person must do.

We may not feel loved, but the source of love is within us. If we look within with an open mind and an open heart, we will find it, for the spiritual treasure — the divine spark — inheres in each one of us.

If you are poor, you just haven't found your treasure yet. Many rich people started with just a dollar or two. Instead of feeling sorry for themselves and living as disempowered victims, they learned to believe in themselves and to multiply what they have. You must learn to do the same.

Jesus told us "What I can do, you can do and more." Why would the master tell us that the source of love and abundance is within each of us, unless it were true?

If we don't listen to the words of the master, whose words are we going to hear? Would we rather listen to the cries of the wounded child and identify with him or her, consigning ourselves to a life of victimhood where life is suffering and never gets better? Is this the message we choose to hear?

The ego cannot save itself. The wounded child cannot bring love to himself. Love comes from a deeper Source. It doesn't matter what we call it.

Call it God. Call it Holy Spirit. Call it the Higher Self. Call it Tao or Essence, or Buddha Nature. It does not matter. But whatever you call it, understand that if your heart is open, it is as near to you as your next breath. Yet if your heart is closed, it as far away as the furthest star.

All this depends on you and you alone. You are the one who stands at the threshold. You decide whether to open your heart or close it down. You are the one who chooses to bring love, or to withhold it.

CHAPTER NINE

Who You Are

If you really knew who you are, then you would not have to look so hard to find the Source of love. You would understand that the Source of love is within you. That is the great truth of Gnosticism: God is Within.

But if you feel unworthy and unlovable, this truth will completely escape you. It doesn't matter how many spiritual teachers you gather around you. You can have Jesus, and Buddha, and Krishna, and Moses, and Muhammed, and all the other luminaries. The white light in the room can be so intense that it illumines all the shadows in the universe, but none of this will matter if you identify with your shadow or project it.

You have the power to make the room go dark.

If you don't accept the light for yourself, it does not exist for you. That is how powerful you are.

God gave you free will. That prodigious gift gave you the choice of living in heaven or living in hell.

God did not say "You have to live in heaven." S/he just

said "Heaven is a great place, but you decide where you want to live."

God is a wise creative Being. S/he knew that you would never internalize the light if you were not able to choose it. S/he knew that you would have to experience the darkness to embrace the light. So S/he said "Okay, so be it. Let the humans have their journey of discovery." And S/he separated the light from the darkness and the waters from the firmament.

Instead of creating an indivisible world. S/he created a world of duality. Of course, S/he knew that dualistic world was not real, but S/he also knew that human beings could make it real, and while they did, they would feel separate from their creator.

But God did not abandon us or leave us stranded in a dark dualistic world. S/he put her creative spark in us. S/he sowed the seed of love ever so deeply within our hearts, knowing that one day it would grow, catch fire and illuminate our world.

So be sure that however dark your world seems, the presence of God, the light and the love of God, dwells in you and with you. If you call out to it, if you pray with all of your heart, the inner light will grow and illuminate your path.

That is God's promise and Her Gift. It is up to you to realize it.

AWAKENING AND REDEMPTION

So how then do we go from feeling unloved to finding the Source of love within us? How do we walk through our shame and fear and rediscover our God-given innocence and our power?

First, we take our mask off and acknowledge our pain. And then we ask for help.

Why is asking for help necessary? First, because nothing can happen in our lives unless we want it to and give our permission. And second, because the wounded child cannot bring love to him or herself. The ego cannot redeem us.

S/He who believes in the darkness cannot bring the light. Only the one who knows and experiences the light can bring it.

So within our consciousness right now we have both the light and the darkness. Denying the light keeps us in victim consciousness. Denying the darkness invalidates the experience of the wounded child whose cries of pain can be heard through the night.

Within our consciousness right now we have the one who feels unloved and unworthy and the one who is connected to love and is capable of bringing it.

How do we move out of the dualistic world? Not by choosing one extreme over the other. We move out of dualism by accepting both poles of our experience: high and low, light and dark, innocence and shame, love and fear.

The wounded child must be willing to accept the love that he craves from the spiritual adult and the spiritual adult must feel compassion for the child who is in pain. Each must accept and work with the other. This relationship between the spiritual adult and the wounded child needs to be cultivated. As that happens, synthesis occurs and healing happens in the psyche.

Psychologically, the split between the opposites must be bridged or we have some kind of dissociation or schizophrenia. Acceptance of divergent aspects of the psyche leads to an energetic exchange and the possibility of integration.

Within the world of spiritual belief, there is another piece of integration that is necessary. Gnosticism suggests that God is within us. The Kabbalah also tells us of the spark of light within each one of us and the journey of the Shekinah — God's chariot of light — through the darkness of the world.

But this is only half of the picture. Yes, God is within us, but God is not within our ego structure. God is not in the shadow or the persona.

The commandments that Moses brought down from Mount Sinai make it clear that we are not to create idols. We are not to make graven images of God. We must not think that God is something that we can picture or define. God is without limits and beyond definition. God always lies just beyond our conscious understanding. That is why He is a mystery.

So we can meet God and experience God as Moses did, but we can never fully know Him. Or, to put it differently, we can know God only with the consciousness that we have at the time. As our consciousness expands, our understanding of God gets deeper and wider. The more we develop a relationship with God, the more He reveals Himself and His truth to us.

To think that we already have the truth, that we already know who and what God is, is the essence of spiritual pride. We need to stand back and become humble.

The schizophrenic may think that he is God and that everyone else is evil, but his thinking is delusional. Fundamentalists of every religion think their religion alone understands the truth about God and that everyone else is a "heathen," but their thinking is also delusional.

If we make God small, then our spirituality will simply become a tool of the ego and we will use it as an excuse to attack other individuals and groups.

No, God cannot be made to fit into any of our boxes. God is beyond the box.

On the other hand, if we see God as separate from us and beyond our capacity to connect with Him, then we begin to despair, because there is no one there to bring love to the child who is in pain.

Making God too big or too small, too close or too far away, reinforces the division in the psyche and increases the potential for individual and collective dissociation.

Then the wounded child tries to bring love to himself and fails miserably, or he believes that love is beyond his reach. Either outcome is unfortunate and unnecessary.

Words and concepts can point us to the truth or away from it. Dualistic words and concepts tend to make it hard for us to understand and heal.

But when we use the language of synthesis and integration, truth becomes more understandable and accessible.

TRAUMA AND HEALING

In the womb it is dark and consciousness is primitive. When the fetus suffers trauma, it goes deep. Wounds suffered in utero may not become accessible. Just the pain is there, without context or reason.

When we are beaten, abandoned, or sexually abused early in our lives, we feel overwhelmed and often repress the memories. We simply cannot process what happened. Later in life when we are stronger and know how to protect ourselves, memories of what happened may come up for healing.

It isn't surprising that those who have been savagely or repeatedly abused don't want to look inside of themselves. Everything is pretty dark there. There are fathoms of fear and shame.

When they seek the light, it makes sense that they seek it outside of themselves. If they are lucky they find a loving role model, a teacher, healer or therapist who acts like the "good mommy" or "good daddy." However, therapists and other healers must be aware of the power of transference. They need to realize that their clients may make them into authority figures and have difficulty taking their power back. Like a good mommy, the doctor, therapist, or healer must take the time to "wean the baby from the breast." If that does not happen, regression can occur, since healing cannot progress unless and until the individual is empowered to take responsibility for bringing love and acceptance to himself.

The danger of surrogate relationships is that the person in authority takes advantage of the vulnerability of the client and old wounds are triggered and shame is reinforced. This happens not only in a therapeutic context, but also in a religious one, where people give their power to priests who abuse them or to charismatic leaders who take their money and use the power of the group or cult to shame them into obedience and submission.

Only when the victims of trauma are convinced that they are not going to find an external savior, do they realize that the only way out of their pain is to begin to walk through it. Hopefully, they do not attempt to make this journey alone, but find a loving, supportive community where they can heal with others who have similar wounds.

Alcoholics and drug addicts are fortunate to have 12 step programs available, where they are surrounded by others who understand their pain and care about their well-being. Sponsors often become a lifeline helping them stay sober or clean until they can address the deeper levels of fear and shame that made them drink or use drugs.

Without the support of caring friends and a compassionate community, it is difficult to heal both our wounds and our addictions. While it is true that the desire to heal must come from each one of us, the inner journey of healing and redemption is made a great deal easier when we have the support of other brothers and sisters and the guidance of those who have made the journey before us.

RECLAIMING OUR INNOCENCE

No matter what we have done, no matter what has happened to us, we are innocent, not guilty. Dark clouds may gather around us, difficult experiences may come our way, but the light remains within us. Our job is to see that light and nurture it.

I know it is hard to love yourself when others do not love you. It is hard to affirm your self-worth when others judge or attack you. But if you don't do it, if you do not rescue yourself from blame, shame and self pity, who is going to do it?

Whether you see God within or God without, is it possible that this God loves you even when you do not love yourself? And if S/He loves you, then can you lean into that love and learn to love yourself?

Even when your friends, your partner, and your family have abandoned you, is it possible that God is still standing at your side? Is God your friend and your companion regardless of the ups and downs of your life?

If so, lean into Him or Her. Open your heart and let the love and light of that eternal Friend shine through.

If God is not your friend and your comforter, if God is the judge who finds fault with you and wants to punish you, then you have accepted a false god. Neither the wounded child nor his abuser can be the comforter.

So take him off the altar. That god is not going to show up for you in any kind of helpful way. Better to have no god, then to have a god who wants to punish you.

Let me tell you a secret. I will whisper it into your ear: "You don't need God to heal. All you need is the memory of your own innocence." Hold onto that and the darkness around you will gradually fall away.

Put your trust in that One. He or She is the One who sleeps by your bed and holds the door open for you when it is time for you to walk through it.

A SIMPLE PRAYER

Dear God Whoever You Are,
I know that you are here to support me
when all outside support falls away.

I know that you are here to love me
when I forget how to love myself.

I know that whatever I do or say,
whatever others do or say to me,
you will still see me and accept me as I am.

When I feel shame, you will remind me
that I am innocent.

When I feel fear, you will help me
hold my fear compassionately
and remind me that I am safe.

When I am being hard on myself or others,
you will help me to soften and be more gentle.

When I feel weak and forlorn,
you will strengthen me and lift my spirit up.

When I am attached, you will help me let go.

When I am lost or distracted,
you will guide me back on track.

When I want to give up,
you will encourage me to persevere.

When I want to die, you will help me
find the courage to live
and to learn from my experience.

Though all others come and go,
You are always here for me.
For that I am so grateful.

CHAPTER TEN

Who Your God Is

In order to move through our pain and transcend our suffering, each one of us needs to enter into a partnership with the God of our understanding. Whether you see God in your heart of hearts and meet Him in the inner temple, or you see God in nature and meet Him on a steep mountain path or on a deserted beach, whether you see God as the energy of love or as your faithful Friend, as the Sufis do, your relationship with Him is paramount.

Some of us call God "He" because we relate to Him as a loving Father. Some of us call God "She" because we relate to Her as a loving Mother.

God is both the great Creator and the great Nurturer. Both Divine Mother and Divine Father are aspects of God, but God Itself is beyond male or female.

We — the reflections or extensions of God — were also created male and female. Adam makes no sense without Eve. Yet we cannot be characterized or defined by our sex any more than God can be. Every man and every woman has both masculine and feminine energy.

Within all dualities, there is a movement toward integration and synthesis. Otherwise we would live in a static universe.

Perhaps that is why many Eastern traditions see God as a Trinity.

In the Taoist Tradition, God is both male and female, both Yang and Yin, but these polar opposites are seen in a dynamic relationship with each other. Yang has Yin within it and Yin has Yang within it, and each is in the process of becoming the other. This dynamic integration and ongoing movement is symbolized in the Tai Chi symbol.

In the Hindu tradition, there are three aspects of God. God is Brahma (the Creator), Vishnu (the Preserver), and Shiva (the Destroyer). This personification of the Divine emphasizes the ongoing nature of creation through its cycles of birth, death and re-birth.

INHERENCE

In Genesis, God looked at His Creation and admired His handiwork. "It is good," He declared. That original goodness inheres in all of us and stays with us throughout our journey here, regardless of our experience of the world.

No matter how badly we feel, no matter how intensely we put ourselves down or trash each other, we do not lose our true identify. To live, to survive, to grow, we must turn toward the God of our understanding and reaffirm our goodness.

Psalm 23 reminds us that God is always with us. He is

like a father for David. David is intimate with Him. That is why he spoke to Him like this:

> Lord, you [1] are my shepherd (my guide)
> and that is why I do not lack for anything.

When David is tired, stressed out or overwhelmed, God helps him find places where he can be nurtured and uplifted:

> You invite me to lie down in green pastures.
> You lead me beside the still waters. You restore my soul.

When David feels challenged by others, he is helped to see them as they really are.

> You lead me in the paths of goodness for your name's sake.

And when difficult times come and David is forced to walk through the dark valley of his fears, he is reminded that there is no place in his heart or his mind where God is not with him.

> Even though I walk through the valley
> of the shadow of death, I fear no evil, for you are with me.
> Your rod and your staff they comfort me.

When dangers appear and resources are scarce, David celebrates God's love, protection and abundance:

> You prepare a table before me in the presence of my enemies.
> You anoint my head with oil. My cup runs over.

---

[1] Note: I have changed the pronoun to underscore the intimacy of the relationship.

David relates to God as a son relates to a caring father, with gratitude for all that has been given to him and hope for the future.

Surely goodness and mercy shall follow me
all the days of my life, and I will dwell in your house forever.

The question is: "Can you and I relate to the God of our understanding with the kind of intimacy and trust that David has with his God? Do we know that our God also walks with us through all of the hills and valleys of our life?"

You see, it does not matter so much how you define God. What matters more is the quality of your relationship with Him or Her. Does your God lead you back to your heart? Does S/he help you find the source of love within and offer it out to others?

Some of you don't like the word God. So be it. Maybe you like the word "angel" or "guide," "higher power" or "higher self." Choose whatever name you like for your shepherd. The name is not important. What is important is where your guide is leading you.

Jesus told us that we will know the worth of a man or woman by his/her fruits. What are the fruits that hang from your tree? Does your faith lead you toward forgiveness and reconciliation or away from it? Does your teacher show you how to love unconditionally or does "her love" lift you up at the expense of others?

Is the fruit that hangs from your tree ripe or rotten? If it is rotten, throw it away. It should not be eaten by you or anyone else.

A spiritual man or woman walks her talk. Her words and actions are congruent. She does not speak out of both sides of her mouth. She does not use truth as a dagger or a whip. She treats others as she wishes to be treated, without exception.

If love is what we have to offer, then we can offer it only in a loving way. If our words and actions are spoken and performed in an unloving manner, then it is not love that is being offered.

Whoever your God is, S/he must be real and transcendent. Many people create gods just to promote their ego agenda. It's only a matter of time before their fruit begins to stink and it is obvious that someone or something is full of shit.

Remember, God may be within, but God is not part of your ego structure. The god of the ego is a hypocrite, a fraud, an imposter, a wolf in sheep's clothing. It is only a matter of time before that god is unmasked and seen for what he or she is.

PART THREE

Bread and Forgiveness

CHAPTER ELEVEN

Our Daily Bread

Like David, Jesus was a man of faith and the prayers he gave to us are powerful. In the Lord's Prayer, Jesus asks God not only for "our daily bread." He also asks God to "forgive our trespasses as we forgive those who have trespassed against us."

Forgiving others is our part in the co-creative relationship. Jesus reminds us that we must do our part to end our suffering.

Of course, in a perfect world, there is no trespass. No one attacks or wounds anyone else. So there is no need for forgiveness.

But in this dualistic world where we think that "our good" and the "good of our brother or sister," are *not* one and the same, trespass is a reality. Someone is always trying to take something from someone else against his will.

This part of suffering is our problem and our responsibility. "Forgiveness," Jesus tells us, is the pathway from trespass to reconciliation.

While we cannot force others to forgive us for what we did to them, we each have the choice to forgive others for what they did to us. Of course, this is not an easy thing to do. And, as I have said many times, we cannot forgive before we are ready. But when we are ready to forgive, we can take our brother or sister off the hook. We can lessen the burden of his guilt and help him to re-affirm his innocence.

Of course, Jesus knows that while we may have been able to forgive others for their trespasses, our brother or sister may not be ready or willing to forgive us. So Jesus asks for God's help. He asks God, who sees us as we truly are, to help us forgive ourselves, for he knows that self-forgiveness is the hardest part of the forgiveness process.

The Lord's Prayer reminds us that not only do we need bread, our support and supply, we also need forgiveness for any misuse of our creative power. For, ultimately, no one can hurt another and benefit himself. If there is any apparent benefit in mistreating others it is short lived, and the pain we cause others invariable returns to us many times over.

FORGIVING OTHERS

Forgiving others benefits us as much as it does them. By forgiving others, we can release ourselves from anger and bitterness and end any tendency we have to attack them back. When forgiveness replaces retribution, the cycle of violence is broken.

If we want to live an empowered life, we must let go of our resentment and stop withholding our forgiveness and our love. For what we withhold from others, is often withheld from us. It is a simple truth that what goes around comes around.

If we don't forgive, how can we receive forgiveness? The heart that opens to give also opens to receive, but the heart that shuts down cannot give or receive.

Withhold forgiveness and you not only condemn your brother. You also condemn yourself. You take a small wound and make it bigger.

When you forgive another person, you not only take your brother off the hook. You take yourself off the hook. You remove the guilt on both sides of the equation.

MAKING AMENDS

Making amends and asking others to forgive our trespasses are natural and necessary steps in the process of healing and atonement. Of course, we must ask in a heart-felt way and show genuine remorse for our unkind words and actions. If we do, we can work through the guilt that comes with every trespass against others.

When we don't apologize for hurting others, we justify our unkind words and actions and make no attempt to correct our mistakes. That locks in our guilt and it makes it more likely that others will hold resentment toward us. Everyone loses when we are afraid to admit our errors and make amends to the people we have hurt.

If we do not ask for forgiveness, we are unlikely to receive it, and then it will be even more difficult for us to forgive ourselves. Together we either build a culture of guilt and punishment or a culture of correction and forgiveness.

It takes a great soul — like a Gandhi or a M.L. King — to turn the other cheek, to offer love in the face of fear, to offer forgiveness in the face of attack or retaliation.

As long as we hold onto our bitterness and resentment, as long we withhold forgiveness from others, and they withhold it from us, we will not find peace in our hearts or in our world. The practice of giving and receiving forgiveness lifts up the heart of every man, woman and child and brings the Peace of God into this world.

THE BODY OF TRUTH

Jesus told us "Man does not live by bread alone, but by every word that comes out of the mouth of God." Hearing and speaking the truth is as important as filling our belly.

Later as he broke bread with his disciples, he told them "Take this and eat … it is my body."

Every profound teaching can and must be internalized. It cannot simply be parroted by those who use the words of others as a crutch. When teachings become empty platitudes they lose their energy and purpose and eventually die out.

The words of Jesus survive because we take them to heart and live them in our lives. We learn to speak from the heart and to walk our talk.

Words without actions that support them are not to be trusted. Only when we do what we are asking others to do can we successfully model the teaching.

The body of Christ is the community that keeps the teachings of Jesus alive. It is the manna made manifest through us. It is the nourishment for both the body and the soul that was given by Moses to the Jews crossing the desert, and the bread that Jesus divided and shared with his disciples.

Truth is given into our hearts and hands. When we internalize it, it becomes part of us and we become part of It. There is a synergy that happens that is both personal and transpersonal.

It is up to each one of us to assimilate and stand up for the teachings we have accepted as the truth. It does not matter if we are Jewish or Christian, Muslim or Hindu, or Buddhist. The words of our prophets and teachers either live in us and through us, or they die.

CHAPTER TWELVE

Prayers Around
the Ceremonial Fire

It is night on the banks of the Euphrates River where a handful of women and men have come to pray. They gather around the ceremonial fire. In the distance you can hear the dim sounds of shells exploding and see stray lights in the sky suddenly go dim like shooting stars. As they pray, there a great moan that seems to come from the river. At first it is barely audible, but it grows in intensity until it reverberates all around the group as they pray.

A few days ago, the one who had once been a loud mouth and a braggart, the Muslim man who had been called to love and inspired brotherhood among all of us, turned to his wife and said "It is time for me to go. God is calling me home. He has something he wants me to do."

Days later another group of women and men were dancing when the drumbeat became fast and furious. They did not question the sound but danced on. Those who had been seeking love were met by a rain of bullets.

As the river spoke, the men and women who had come to pray, heard a gentle voice speaking through the thunder of the waves. "Do not be afraid,' It said. "Death is just a doorway. Walk through this door, brothers and sisters. I came here before you to welcome you and to guide you home."

And they saw the bodies lifted out of the river, riding the song of the waves, and they heard him talking to them gently, reassuring them that there was nothing to fear. And then they heard him speak to the man who pulled the trigger, who was hiding in the shadows.

"You come too," he said. "God isn't happy with you, but He knows you are not a bad man. You just need more love than the rest of us." And he hoisted the killer up onto his back and rose like an eerie mist into the sky.

The people who gathered by the ceremonial fire could hardly believe what they saw, but they knew that somehow an angel had appeared amongst them.

Then they heard another voice that shook the heavens. "That was Ali," It said. "His name means "high" and when I gave it to him I told him "You are not here just to lift yourself up. You are also here to lift up all of your brothers and sisters."

And they began to chant: "Ali, Ali, Ali, As in life, so in death." And they watched him disappear into the mist, until nothing could be seen except the dark dome of the heavens and the stars falling through the night sky.

A TIME TO MOURN

In life there is joy and sadness, a time to celebrate and a time to mourn. The great ones come and go and the ones who need the most love sometimes take it indiscriminately. We are not going to change the world around us, at least not for a long time. Meanwhile, we can work on changing our own mind and holding our fears and those of others compassionately.

The powerful thing about grieving is that it brings us all back together. It brings us back into our hearts where we are called to stand up for the gifts and values of the beloved and keep them alive.

Ali was a not just a boxer. He was a fighter, who stood up against injustice. He stood up for the right to be himself, to be heard and respected. He did not fit the mold of greatness known at the time. He made us uncomfortable. He challenged us to grow. We simply could not ignore him or dismiss him.

He was persistent. He was unpredictable. He was dazzling. No matter how many clouds gathered over his head, his light continued to shine.

We had no choice but to see him and listen to him.

In claiming his own right to shine, he claimed ours as well. It did not matter if we were black or white, Jewish or Muslim, straight or gay. All of us have the right, indeed the responsibility to be who we are authentically in this world.

So we celebrate his victory and we mourn the loss of those who stood up to be seen and were greeted by bullets. God knows it is not the first time.

The price of freedom is sometimes death. Does that mean that we will be intimidated and refuse to stand up to violence and oppression? Or will it stiffen our resolve?

Some people kill because they feel hurt, abandoned, or ostracized and there is hatred in their hearts. They feel that no one sees them or cares about them. They try to force us to take notice, but then of course it is too late.

Even as a child the killer acted out in negative ways to try to get attention. He threatened others. He pushed people away. As an adult, he abused his wife and was fired from many jobs. People could feel the anger in him and they avoided him as much as possible.

Confused about his sexuality and afraid to accept the possibility that he was gay, he began casing gay bars at the same time that he was visiting Jihadist websites. For him power and powerlessness commingled.

Homophobia and terrorism were a perfect match.

He was a time bomb that was quietly ticking. He was interviewed by the FBI several times, as were other assassins who came before him. They heard the clock ticking, but they didn't realize it was a bomb. It's ironic that the ones who specialize in finding bombs don't know anything about triggers.

This happens over and over again. Find someone who feels unloved, who feels ignored, or cast out and you find another ticking clock.

"But we didn't find any explosives," law enforcement says and, of course, they are right. But explosives are easy to find when the clock says "It's time."

Without the trigger, there can be no bomb, so we have

to look for the trigger. We have to identify those who are at risk and will in a matter of time put others at risk.

We have to identify those who feel unloved, rejected, abandoned, not seen and not heard. And we have to intervene before it is too late. That is a very big job.

That is not just the job of every law enforcement officer. It is the job of every teacher, every counselor, every caseworker, every doctor, nurse or co-worker. It is your job and my job.

Muhammad knew that. That is why he was always reaching out to others. Maybe now we can finally hear what he came to tell us.

CHAPTER THIRTEEN

Taking Ourselves Off the Cross

In the end, we can forgive others and they can forgive us, but we still have a hard time forgiving ourselves. There is still part of us that feels bad and unworthy. There is still a part of us that believes that we should be punished and we can be very hard on ourselves.

It isn't easy for us to come off the cross and let go of our guilt. In some way, we identify with our suffering. We become attached to the drama of sin and guilt.

We don't know what it is like to live without the drama. We don't know what it is like to be innocent.

Perhaps we believe that when the drama of shame and blame ends, the world will end with it and that really scares us. We don't know if it is really possible to have Heaven on earth.

Jesus told us "The meek will inherit the earth." When the swords have been turned into plowshares, when each person knows that his good and that of his brother are one and the same, when poverty and injustice come to an end, what will the world be?

If there was anyone who had to learn to forgive God surely it had to be Job. God hit Job with one ferocious thunderbolt after another. He scorched the ground under Job's feet. His attack on his faithful son seemed to be merciless. And He didn't treat Jesus all that well either.

If God did not show up the way Job and Jesus expected Him too, it isn't likely that He is going to show up the way you or I expect. God has His own agenda, His own timetable.

Or, maybe as my friend Khadra suggests "God does not care." Once He created us, He just disappeared. He isn't even standing on the sidelines rooting for us.

Throughout history, human beings have been maimed and brutalized, usually at each other's hands. Is that God's fault? Or is it ours?

No matter how you answer that question, there is a major piece of work to do.

Elisabeth Kubler-Ross told me about the time she was with a medical team that accompanied the Allied forces when they liberated the concentration camps. She saw the twisted faces and the emaciated bodies and she asked, "How could they do that to people?"

One of her colleagues, an older Jewish woman, replied "You would do it too."

Of course, Elisabeth did not believe her. A couple of weeks later she was hitch-hiking home through Austria or Switzerland. She was tired and thirsty and she had not eaten for days. She saw a child approaching with a crust of bread. And she had an enormous desire to grab that crust of bread from the child and eat it. And she knew in that moment that the older Jewish woman was right.

All of us are guilty. There isn't anything that anyone has done that we under the same circumstances would not do. So how can we judge?

Jesus asked the mob that had gathered to stone the prostitute: "Who will throw the first stone?"

No matter what you think the world is and how you think it will end or transform, one thing is clear. Some of us are not going to be saved while the rest of us are left to burn in the fires of hell. I know a lot of people still believe that, but they have bad information.

If we are going to survive and thrive, we will survive and thrive together. And, if not, we will suffer the same ugly and unfortunate fate.

Our fate and that of our brother and sister are intricately entwined. No one, not even God or Satan, can separate the threads.

When the nails were pounded into his body, Jesus told his executioners, "I forgive you because you know not what you do." Even at the end, when he was experiencing the most intense pain, he told us

"Forgiveness is the only way."

Can we forgive our brother and sister for hurting us? Can we forgive ourselves for hurting them? Can God forgive us for making such a mess? Can we forgive God for not showing up?

These are humbling and important questions. Each one of us, in our own unique way, came here to find the answers.

GRABBING THE BULL BY THE HORNS

We all have to start somewhere. If you are facing the bull, you can't pretend he isn't there or turn and run away. If you do, he will make fast work of you.

If you don't take the bull by the horns, you might have to try to take him by the tail, and then you will get the shit kicked out of you.

Nobody likes to face those horns, but there is no way around it. You need to show the bull that you are not afraid, even if you are.

Your salvation depends on you. It depends on the choices that you make or refuse to make.

David was afraid too when he was facing Goliath. But he stood his ground. To be sure, the odds were not in his favor. And the same is true for us.

The odds say that we won't succeed. But not succeeding is not an option.

There is an old saying: "God never gives us more than we can bear." Another way of saying this is "We can bear a lot more than we think we can."

Victor Frankl told us the Nazis could beat him, humiliate him and take his freedom away, but they could not control his heart or his mind. No matter what they said or did to him, his innocence remained unstained.

If it is true that our suffering never exceeds our capacity to bear it and learn from it, then life can only make us stronger and more determined to succeed.

We will reach within to find the courage to face the obstacles and adversity that life brings. We will move through our pain, whatever it looks like, for as long as it lasts.

When we are willing to stand and face our fears, we find the courage and resilience that are required to succeed. On the other hand, when we are intimidated or overwhelmed by our fears, we do not come to know the strength we have.

Many of us think that we would be better off if the bull never came into our lives. But think about it. Who would David have become without Goliath?

He would have become a man like other men. He would not have become the King of the Jews.

Those who inspire us to greatness are those who overcome obstacles and challenges, not those who play it safe and try to avoid them.

Whatever trials or tribulations you face, know that they are there to make you stronger and to give you the tools that you need to live an inspired life. They are not here to beat you down or punish you.

If you believe in God, choose a loving God who wants you to shine your light and offer your gifts to the world. And when challenges come, welcome them, for they are here to make you stronger and wiser.

110   Paul Ferrini

PART FOUR

Trusting the
Universe

CHAPTER FOURTEEN

Being Present

So if you were not vanquished by the bull, there must be a reason why you are still standing there. Maybe God has a plan for you. Or maybe, if Khadra is right, God doesn't care, and it's just a scary coincidence. Either way, you must have work to do, or you wouldn't be there.

Maybe you were in an accident and you were the only survivor. Or maybe you defied the odds and healed yourself of some incurable disease.

When you experience something poignant, awesome, or miraculous, it gets your attention and it gets the attention of others.

Whatever was true for you before you experienced that event might not be true after it. Or it might be more true and more compelling.

Before David slew Goliath, he was just a boy going nowhere in particular. But at the moment Goliath fell, David's job description changed. He wasn't trying to change it. It just happened.

Life often unfolds in strange and unanticipated ways. Sometimes we are called to the plate in the bottom of the ninth inning and we don't even know how to swing a bat. But you know what? It doesn't seem to matter. If you find yourself in that position, then you are meant to be there, even if you don't know how or why.

Who is in charge here, anyway? God or Godot? I know that Godot was not expected to show up, but at the last minute maybe he did. Some people stand around doing nothing and being bored for a very long time and then someone comes along and kicks their ass so hard they actually leave the ground.

Anyway, it's a good thing that life is not predictable. If it was, you wouldn't be here, nor would I, so let's be thankful for the unexpected twist of fate that brought us here, and see what's coming next.

TRUTH WITHOUT A FACE

I know that some of you don't like the word God and think I have wasted a lot of your time talking about God, so I am going to give you a little break. I'm not going to talk about God for a while. I'm going to talk about the universe, just like Stephen Hawking did.

Well, maybe not exactly like he did.

When we talk about universal truth, we can leave the idea of a "personal" God aside. Khadra would like that. After all, if there is a "personal" God and we don't have a relationship with Him then we are really screwed, so we have to be glad to let that one go.

Now all we are working with is the energy and how it behaves.

One of the things that we know about energy is that sometimes it travels in a straight line, from point A to point B. And sometimes it doesn't. Sometimes it moves in a circle or an ellipse, like a planet orbiting the sun, or an electron spinning around the nucleus of an atom.

When we are young we buy into the idea that the journey of life is a linear one. After all, our growth seems to be sequential and continuous. After we are born we grow bigger and learn to move around with greater dexterity. We learn to walk and talk and maybe even drive a car or fly a plane. We have a pretty wide reach for someone who began as a tiny speck inside our mommy's womb.

But as we grow older, we stop getting bigger. In fact, some of us shrink. We begin to slow down and turn inward. Maybe we are retracing our steps. It's hard to know exactly where we are going to end up, but it is clear that the linear aspect of our life no longer prevails.

That's when we realize that we were never really moving in a straight line. We have been moving up and down and all around, just like everyone else.

When we were young, we were motivated to climb the mountain. So we trained hard and got the best equipment and in time we were able to reach the summit. But after reaching the summit, we realized we couldn't stay there. We had to go back down the mountain. The best we could do to make it interesting was to take a different path down.

Climbing the same mountain gets a little old, so we

find other mountains. But in time our energy and excitement fade, and we wonder what else we can do.

So we take up deep sea diving, but eventually we get bored with that too.

So here we are, like Malloy, walking on the beach, shifting the stones from one pocket of our greatcoat to another and wondering what to do with ourselves.

"Is this all there is?" we ask.

And then, for no reason in particular, there is a knock on our door. We open it and an old childhood friend appears and tells us "Time to take the next train for Memphis."

After he delivers the message, he leaves.

Now we have a choice, we are either going to take the next train for Memphis or we aren't.

Let's say we go to Memphis and we find an interesting job working at Graceland. Then we can say "Good choice. I'm really flowing with the energy." But maybe we go to Memphis and nothing happens. So we get back on the train to go home, and out of the train window we see a big sign that says "Pet alligators for sale."

That gets our attention, so we get off the train to check out the pet alligators and we meet this unbelievably attractive woman who tells us "Ain't no alligators here." And we can't take our eyes off her. So we ask

"So what do you have here?"

"All I got here is my Jamaican husband." She answers. And something lights up in the back corner of our brain and we remember that a year ago Khadra told us about her Jamaican husband and how he made off with over two million Euros.

So we call Khadra up and tell her "Time to take the

next train to Memphis." And she responds "Are you serious or is this just a joke?"

And the truth is we don't really know. We are just passing on the information. It's up to her whether she takes it seriously or not.

CULTIVATING DETACHMENT

Bill Shakespeare told us that life is a stage and we are all actors in the play. He might be right. Or maybe there is no play and no playbook.

Or perhaps all of this is a different kind of play, the kind of thing children do when they are having fun. And maybe the only question you need to ask yourself or anyone else is "Are you having fun?"

If the answer is "Yes," then you might have found the best way out of suffering. Even Gautama would be jealous. And if the answer is "No," maybe you need to stop taking yourself so seriously.

When children "play house," they know they are not the real mommy or daddy. They just pretend to be. So if mommy is being mean to her little child, they aren't really worried because they know it's just a game. It isn't real.

When you know that three dimensional reality and the suffering it entails is just a game, you don't have to buy into the drama. You can detach a bit and just watch what is going on.

You don't even have to buy a ticket on the train to Memphis, because it doesn't matter if you go or not.

In the Bhagavad Gita we are told that the world is changeable and impermanent. To the extent that we are attached to this world, we will suffer. By detaching we are able to do what Jesus asked us to do: "To be in the world without being of the world."

Jesus also told us "Be as little children." Be innocent. Be curious. Explore the world and have fun. We can do all of that quite well if we are not attached to the outcome.

Our suffering begins when we start taking all of this too seriously, when we become invested in what happens or how it happens. Then we can actually fool ourselves into thinking that we can control the outcome. And when it turns out that we can't, we get back up on the cross or put a pistol in our mouth.

That's how crazy the drama gets.

Our ego's persistent attempt to control our experience is guaranteed to fail. We are just one of many actors in the play. We aren't writing it or directing it.

In the end, it is not our experience itself that matters so much as how we hold our experience. Since we can't control what happens, that is a good thing.

Our job is just to show up for what happens and to be as gentle as we can be to ourselves and others.

Here are a few mantras that can help remind you.

- Life is constantly changing. This too will pass.

- I don't know what anything means.

- Things are not always as they appear to be.

- How I hold my experience is more important than what happens.

- Solemnity is over-rated. Can I see the humor in this?

- Can I lighten up and stop taking myself (and others) so seriously?

- I can be present without judging or taking sides.

- I can love myself (and you) right now in this moment.

- I can feel compassion for all beings who are in pain, including myself.

COOPERATING WITH THE ENERGY

The universal energy is like a river. It moves with an undercurrent. In times of monsoon, the river rises and the current intensifies. Floods can occur. Yet in times of drought, the river dwindles and slows. If you are going to go out on the river, you have to be observant. You have to see what the river is doing.

If you live by the sea and you want to launch your boat, you can't do it at low tide, because there isn't enough water for the boat to float. You have to wait for high tide. You have to be patient and work with the energy that is available.

If you want to sail, you have to wait for the wind to pick up, but if the wind is too intense you may be in for a scary ride.

Your life also has its own trajectory and flow and it is important that you tune into it. Living in your own creative flow is essential if you are going to move away from suffering and realize your full potential.

If you try to make something happen, you won't succeed, or if you do succeed it will not be much fun. People who swim against the current or row against the tide usually get exhausted fairly quickly and have little energy left to do the really important things in life.[2]

[2] For more information about working with cycles, please read my book *Having the Time of Your Life*.

HAVING THE TIME OF YOUR LIFE

Ecclesiastes tells us "There is a time for every purpose under heaven." There is a time to rest and a time to act. Acting when it is time to rest cannot be successful. You will wear yourself out. But resting when it is time to act is equally dysfunctional. You will squander important opportunities.

When we don't take the time to rest when we need to recharge or when we don't seize the moment when the right moment comes, we stay locked into our patterns of self-betrayal.

ON THE BANKS OF THE RIVER

You may not believe in God, but you better believe in the River because you are probably living on it or beside it.

Throughout history humans have settled down on the banks of a river or the shores of the sea. They are drawn to water because their bodies are made up mainly of water.

As the rivers flow to the sea, as the tides of the sea rise and recede, so does the blood move in and out from our hearts. And as the moon waxes and wanes all the fluids of the body are engaged and released.

We are part of the universal energy of creation, not just our bodies, but our minds also, and our spirit that each day rises and sets like the sun and measures its time by the stars turning in the sky and the shifting seasons.

Yes, there is a time to plant and a time to reap, a time to gather and a time to disperse. We come here not to have dominion over the earth, as Genesis suggests, but to learn from the earth so that we can live in the universal flow and walk in the footsteps of our ancestors.

There is an intimacy here indigenous people know and the rest of us have forgotten. But if we are listening to the song of the river as it flows by, we will begin to remember.

We may feel alone and cut off from others, but we are not alone and we cannot be cut off from the Mother who nurtures and sustains us until the storms come. The river runs through our blood. It swells in our thighs. It brings us children and carries them away at flood time.

There is no part of us that is not touched. All of us have been loved and beaten, pulled in and cast away.

We have been softened and made more vulnerable. God may not make us humble, but the River does.

PATIENCE, HUMILITY, DETACHMENT

Wisdom comes not just from the battles we have won, but also from the battles we have lost.

Fortunately for us, the ego does not win its perpetual campaign to take charge of our lives. In the end, we come to realize that progress on the path is not linear and we have to come back again and again to the lessons life would have us learn.

Most of us have to bang our head against the wall repeatedly before we realize that we are not here to be a battering ram, but to learn to walk through the open doors.

That requires patience. Sometimes we have to wait a long time before the door opens. If we are impatient we will pass by the door and we won't see when it opens. Then we will have to retrace our steps and wait some more.

It helps if we realize that we don't know how or why anything happens.

That is true even if we are clear about our goal.

Being clear about your goal, knowing what you want or need, is helpful. Thinking you know how the goal will be reached or how your needs will be met is not helpful.

Many people tell us "Let go and let God." And if you don't trust anyone called God then "Let go and let the universe." After all, Einstein told us that the universe is friendly.

The goal and the process are different. The process is forever unknown and inscrutable. Whenever you think you know how the universe works, it throws you a curve ball. Whenever you come to the plate complacent, you strike out. You have to be alert and on your toes.

You have to pay close attention. And even when you are alert, you can still strike out. And then you will have to be humble and patient and wait for the next at-bat. If you get angry at yourself or the pitcher, you will squander your next opportunity.

The one thing that the universe tells you that is very helpful is this: "It isn't personal, so don't take it personally." The universe did not single you out for praise or punishment.

Sometimes you are in the universal flow and sometimes you are not.

That's not just true for you. It is true for everybody.

The best thing you can do is to realize when you are in the flow and then trust it and let go. That seems to work pretty well. With the universe behind you the goal can be reached quickly and without struggle. It's pretty obvious that you are in the flow when you have hit three or four three point shots in a row.

On the other hand, it is also helpful to realize when you are not in the flow. If you have missed three or four consecutive three point shots, it might be time to pass the ball to your teammates.

Great athletes know when they are in the zone and they learn to trust it. You and I need to learn to do the same.

Whether you are a basketball player or an astrophysicist, the same rules apply.

Remember, when you are in the flow, let go and trust the universe. When you are not in the flow, focus on defense and pass the ball to someone else.

In the end, we need patience, humility and detachment to succeed. Even the best players in the world have a slump once in a while, or a bad game or two. You can't force yourself back into the flow. You just have to show up and be willing.

Your best strategy for weathering the down times is:

- Don't beat yourself up.

- Don't blame anyone else.

- Let the past go.

- Let your expectations go.

- Just show up and be willing.

- Accept what is.

- Repeat these steps.

When you know how fierce the river can be, it isn't easy to trust it. But maybe trust is not the real issue here. When you know the river you learn to respect it. You see how it can help you reach your goal, and you also see how it can destroy everything you have.

If you have a choice, you build on higher ground. If not, you listen carefully to the current and the changing wind. You never take the river for granted, one way or the other.

The river has no other intent but to flow to the sea. Sometimes its flow is turgid and mighty and it wipes out everything in its path. Sometimes it slows to a trickle or becomes calm like a lake. The river has many moods. It is like you and I in that respect.

When we respect the power of the river, we have a healthy relationship with it. We know when it is safe to jump in and trust the current, and when we need to be cautious or wary.

A wise woman or man is vigilant and reads the signs. He or she may not always be right, but s/he is rarely naïve or foolish.

Knowing that the river is more powerful than you are is not a bad thing. Giving the universe a healthy respect helps you avoid a lot of trouble.

The question is "Can we keep a healthy distance and be intimate at the same time?" That is a good question not just for our relationship with the river, but for our relationship with others too.

When the weather is good, we love to dive into the

river and play. When we fall in love we dive into our beloved's arms and throw all caution to the wind.

But the mood of the river can change suddenly. What felt safe can get scary fast.

If we are not careful, we can become enmeshed with others and forget our boundaries. We can take on a responsibility that belongs to them or try to give them a responsibility that belongs to us. Before long, we give away our power. We become trapped in an abusive relationship and have to fight to take our power back.

If we are not careful, falling in love can be a dangerous act. The waters of emotion can rise and overwhelm us. We can drown seeking someone else's love, instead of retreating to the riverbank and finding the love in our own heart.

Real intimacy with each other is no different than intimacy with the river. Without respect and good boundaries, intimacy is at best a temporary phenomenon.

Of course, it's okay occasionally to lose yourself in someone else, as long as you remember to find yourself again. It's okay to jump in the river, as long as you climb out when the winds pick up and the clouds gather overhead.

All this is common sense, and yet we find it so challenging.

We have to remember that we are not each other's savior. We are just reflections of each other. I cannot make you happy and you cannot make me happy. The best we can do is help each other see the love and acceptance we are still withholding from ourselves.

Respecting each other, respecting our relationship, means respecting the differences between us as well as the similarities. It means being humble and patient when we don't agree or share the same desires.

Without mutual respect, how can there be trust? Trust is something that happens when respect has been cultivated consistently. We learn to trust each other when we know that we are capable of forgiving each other for our mistakes. We learn to trust when we suffer pain or loss and see that we are able to heal together, when we see that our relationship, while imperfect, is strong and resilient. We learn to trust when we see that our hearts can open again when they have shut down, when we see we can find each other, even after we have separated or pushed each other away.

Nobody cultivates respect or trust overnight. It is a lifelong process that requires that we learn good boundaries and are willing to forgive each other when those boundaries are crossed.

The river is deep and the river is wide. Sometimes we cross over gently to the other side, and sometimes we capsize and we have to swim for our lives.

That is why we cannot take anything for granted. Even as we celebrate our victories or mourn our defeats, we need to take care for today, for each day brings its own unique challenges.

CHAPTER FIFTEEN

Krishna's Flute

A*Course in Miracles* tell us that we don't need to move mountains or part the waters of the sea. We just need to be willing. "A little willingness" on our part can lead to miraculous results.

Remember, David really didn't want to battle Goliath. But he realized that no one else was going to volunteer. Someone had to confront Goliath, so it might as well be him.

He knew that it was a "long shot," so he was surprisingly calm. Either it would work or it wouldn't.

When we are willing to show up and trust the process, amazing things can happen.

Many of us think that in order to show up we have to first get a PhD and a black belt in Karate, but it usually does not work that way.

It's not that preparation can't be helpful, but often we don't have time to prepare. We have to step forward and meet the challenge in the moment with whatever skill and resources we have.

Like David the boy, most of us are not professional fighters. Our courage is not cultivated. It simply arises when we show up with heart and do the best that we can. The rest depends on the universe. If we are in the flow of life and we trust it, the stone we hurl can find its mark.

When we show up with trust and heart, miracles happen. Yet, while they are done through us, we are not the "doer." We step forward and allow the universal energy to work through us. We don't know the outcome and we have no control over it. All we can do is to show up and be willing.

St. Francis prayed "Lord, make me an instrument of your peace." He was willing to be present and to be used as a vehicle for the divine energy and he did not take credit for what was done through him. He was content to be the hollow reed through which the sound comes.

When we don't need credit, we are content to be the flute in Krishna's hands. There is nothing more wonderful than being the empty vessel through which the universal energy moves. Every mother that gives birth knows the joy of being the vessel, even though the process of giving birth can be challenging.

Is this not what it means to "submit" to the universal energy as it unfolds in your life? Every time you show up and trust, you see amazing things transpire, things that you could never have predicted or imagined.

That is when you realize that there is a wisdom and intelligence that is operating in your life. All you have to do is let go of your need to control and you give it permission to express through you.

As long as your survival needs dominate, you are too

dense to be a vehicle for light or for love. Your ego needs to "be the doer." It needs credit, praise, approval.

Only when you can set all that aside can you open up the channel through which Spirit can flow. Then the most exquisite music can be made through you.

Yet without your willingness to show up, there would be no instrument to play.

The truth is the universe needs you as much as you need it. Energy needs a form through which it expresses.

Be content to be the vehicle, the form, the flute, so that the music of life can be played through you. When the reed is played, it too becomes ecstatic. Then there is no more Krishna or you. There is just the haunting sound of the flute echoing in the canyon.

SILENCE AND SURRENDER

When we allow ourselves to be the vehicle, we surrender to the flow of life.

We don't surrender to a human being. We don't surrender to an ideology. If we do, we just give away our power.

Surrender has nothing to do with giving up your power to an idea or another person. Surrender has nothing to do with personalities, or cults or belief systems.

Surrender has to do with the dissolution and death of the ego. Surrender means we recognize the futility of manipulation or control. We stop trying to make things happen.

We refrain from speaking and acting when there is nothing constructive that we can do or say. Then we do not speak or act in a wound-driven way.

Instead we become silent and aware and we remain in that peaceful state until we are spontaneously called by life to speak or act. And then our words and actions are inspired.

They do not come from our ego consciousness. They arise from the indwelling Universal Energy that abides in us and expresses through us in a unique and authentic way.

Words and actions that arise from the silence of the heart are powerful and compelling. Others cannot help but take notice.

If we want to inspire others, we take the time to cultivate truth within our hearts. We dwell in the silence until there is something important and meaningful to say.

Resting in the heart, abiding in the silence, is a spiritual practice. It is something we do throughout the day. When we find the mind chattering, when we see that we are being drawn into the drama, we pull ourselves back into the heart. We focus on the breath. We quiet the mind.

The more we practice, the more peace and clarity we have. We become like the still waters of the lake reflecting the sunlight and the clouds above.

We become a mirror, instead of the one who parades before it. People come and go, thoughts come and go. They can be seen in the mirror but the mirror is not attached to their coming or going.

Until one day, we are startled by some passing sound or shape, and the wind suddenly picks up, disturbing the quiet surface of the lake.

We notice that too.

In those few rare moments, we are the witness and the one who is being witnessed at the same time.

Our spiritual life begins in the trenches but it ends in the sky where the leaves dance ecstatically in the wind and the birds sing the song of each day as it begins and ends.

When we are no longer afraid of our fear or anyone else's, when we are no longer attached to who we are or what we see, we move gracefully, as the branches move in the wind, their leaves shimmering, in sunlight and shadow.

Soon the flowers will bud and the fruits will gather and fall. Each will give the gifts that he has to give, without hesitation or effort.

That is how it is. It is completely ecstatic.

CHAPTER SIXTEEN

No Prescription

When you are sick, you go to the doctor and s/he prescribes some pills to make you feel better. But if you suffer as most human beings do, not just from some external condition, but from your own thoughts and feelings, there is no doctor or guru who can help you.

Of course, many try. "Just change your thoughts" or "Just feel your feelings," they say, "and your pain will go away." But none of this works.

The more you try to change your thoughts, the more they proliferate. The more you feel your feelings the more you identify with them. If anything, your pain intensifies.

Whatever you identify with or resist just gets stronger. Unfortunately, when you try to stop identifying or stop resisting, the same thing happens.

There isn't any trick that anyone can give you that's going to solve your problem. You just have to see what is happening without judging it, or if you judge it, see the judgment. If you do this, in time your ego will just get completely exasperated and throw the towel in. It is kind of like counting sheep. After you have counted thousands of them, you just get tired and fall asleep.

After all, how many sheep can you count? Everyone has his limits.

Once you see the judgment and the judgment of the judgment, and the judgment of the judgment of the judgment, you realize that you, like everyone else here, are running a judgment factory. When someone comes by your bench and asks you what you are doing, you just tell them "I'm working on my judgments."

You don't make it bad or wrong or unspiritual. You just acknowledge it for what it is.

We all have a lot of sheep to count. But then, one day, after the parade of endless sheep, something arises that is not a sheep.

On the other hand, you may not like counting sheep; you might prefer to play golf. So for you it might happen after playing four hundred rounds of golf.

Everyone wants a prescription, but if I gave you a prescription I would just send you off on another wild goose chase.

I trust that you will find the way that works for you. You may have to wear yourself out thoroughly before the way becomes clear. You might need to get down on your knees and ask for help. But sooner or later, the door will open and you will walk through it.

ALL THE ANSWERS ARE WITHIN

The good news is that all the answers you need are within. The bad news is that this is the last place you are going to look.

So, like most people, you will spend a good deal of your life looking to other people to give you the answers, and they will be only too happy to oblige. You will walk down many crooked paths that take you away from your heart. In the end, like Don Quixote, tired and defeated, you will return home.

You will sit listening to your heart quietly beating, while your restless mind invents new expeditions to fight windmills and save damsels in distress. As long as you watch your thoughts and don't fly out the door to engage in the next battle, your mind eventually calms down.

You begin to realize that this is just a story that you are making up because you are bored and afraid to sit still. You realize that you don't have to keep that story going. You can drop it. You can stop seeking for truth outside yourself.

When the story comes to an end, the story-maker meets him or herself. And that is the moment when things shift.

Then you realize the enormity of your own creative power. You see how you create a universe of suffering and lack from your shame and your fear. And you know that it is better to focus on facing your fears then on saving others or trying to fix the world around you.

As you sit with yourself, you realize that you are okay the way you are. You don't need to be fixed and you don't need to fix anyone else. That takes a huge burden off your shoulders.

Now, you don't have so much to do. You can simplify your job description. Now your job description reads:

"Show up and learn to love and accept yourself as you are."
That is a far cry from saving damsels or fighting windmills.
90% of the drama has been peeled away.

Now there is just a thin skin left on the onion and that
can easily be removed.

SINKING INTO THE CORE SELF

Beneath the running stream of judgments and the alternating current of emotional attachment and resistance is something that is like a solid core. All the other stuff spins around it, like clouds moving through the sky. We call that solidity at the center of our being The Core Self.

It represents what does not change, what is not subject to external conditions. In this unchanging center of our being, love is ever-present and unconditional. Locating that center and anchoring in it as the world spins around us is the purpose of our spiritual aspiration and practice.

Once the drama of shame and blame falls away, once we stop trying to fix ourselves and everyone else around us, we dwell close to that center. We go in and out of it, coming to peace, moving into struggle, and returning to peace again.

Now the thin skin around the onion comes off more easily and we can feel and taste the juices within us. Love is no longer something abstract. It is a palpable reality. It is an energy that moves in us and through us, touching everyone who travels with us.

Love is not something that we seek. It is not something separate from us that we can find in the world. It is who we are.

All of this happens without any great effort on our part. When we live close to the center of our being love is like the air we are breathing. It is an essential energy exchange with the universe.

We spend a lifetime following many circuitous paths, but in the end all paths merge and lead us to the banks of the river. Once we arrive at the river, there is nowhere else to go. There is nothing that we need to say or do. We have reached the destination.

This is scarier for us than we may expect. Who will we be when striving comes to an end, when we are no longer defined from the outside in, by how we look, by what we say or what we do? Will we be able to rest in our Core Self while the river rushes past us, or will we be swept up by the current and taken downstream?

There is in all of us a fear of death, a fear of being swept away, losing our identity, disappearing without a trace. When we are ready we will walk through that fear. We will enter the river and cross to the other side.

There is no rush, no pressure. We can take the time that we need. No one can force us to let go before we are ready.

PART FIVE

Living in Joy

CHAPTER SEVENTEEN

Not Feeding the Tigers

When you come to the end of suffering, you live in joy. You enjoy life as it unfolds before you. Because you are willing, opportunities to learn and to grow present themselves and you engage them. Occasionally, of course, you become attached to the outcome or try to control life as it unfolds and then you experience the old pain and struggle again. That is normal. This is not a linear path.

But now you have a taste of what it means to live in joy and freedom from the past. So you relinquish the old patterns quickly so that you can return to living peacefully in the present.

Now and then, negative thoughts or feelings of unworthiness arise and you witness them without identifying with them. Or perhaps you identify with them for a short time and then realize it and drop it.

Living in joy does not mean that joy is all that you experience. There are plenty of bumps on the road that you will weather. They may disturb you for a while, but they do not throw you off the path.

When you do not interpret events and circumstances in a negative way, you remove at least half of the potential for struggle. If you don't feed the tiger, it does not get bigger and bigger until it has the power to overwhelm you.

Every negative interpretation you make, every feeling of unworthiness you identify with, feeds the tiger. And the more you feed him, the hungrier he gets and the more he can eat.

If you like props, put a sign up on your bathroom mirror that says "Do not feed the tiger." That will remind you that you must be vigilant about negative thoughts and emotions so that you do not sabotage the creative flow of joy in your life.

Remember, living in joy is not hard. It is the natural way to live, so it is easy, indeed effortless. You don't have to push the river. It moves along nicely by itself.

NO MORE SACRIFICE

Just as you say no to your own tiger, you must be willing to say no to other people's tigers. Otherwise you will be complicit in their suffering. When others ask you to do something that does not feel right to you, tell the truth to them and don't feel guilty for doing it.

That way, no tigers are fed, not yours or theirs. That keeps the suffering quotient down so that it is manageable.

There will always be people around who want to sell you something you don't need or get you to subscribe to their campaigns at your expense. Remember Caveat Emptor. Buyer beware.

You are responsible for what you agree to, not the person who sets the bait.

The world of wounded men and women is not a very compassionate or convivial place. The bait is scattered everywhere around you. That isn't a problem if you refuse to bite down on the hook. It is a problem only if you do.

The religion of sacrifice does not support the freedom of women and men. It is just another tiger looking to be fed. It will be happy to have you for lunch if you allow it.

Self-betrayal happens when you say "Yes" to something that does not honor you. And there is a direct link between self-betrayal and suffering. So even when you come to the edge of the river and you understand how you have given your power away in the past, you will still be given opportunities to do so again and again.

These are just tests that reinforce the lessons you have learned. When your "No," is firm, it is respected by others and the tests will get fewer and further between.

The beautiful thing about living in joy and abundance is that is happens naturally. As soon as self-betrayal stops, we return to the flow. It is the default setting on our software.

While it is helpful if you know what you want, it is more important that you know what you don't want. Be clear about that and committed to saying "No" to it and the "Yes" will take care of itself.

The ultimate question for all of us is "Who or What is holding our experience here?" If everything here is held in the compassionate arms of Divine Mother then we are all safe, no matter what occurs. Mistakes may happen. Trespasses may occur. Sadness or pain may arise, but all this is held in loving acceptance and compassion. Being thus contained, it does not have the potential to overwhelm us.

If you are the bringer of love to your own experience, then you are like Divine Mother holding everything in her compassionate embrace. You have created a safe and friendly place within your own consciousness where you can come to terms with what is happening in your life.

Remember, it is not just what is happening that is important. It is how you hold it. Hold it in love and you remain in a state of acceptance and peace.

If fear arises, which it will do, no matter how spiritual you are, you must ask "Can I hold it in compassionate awareness?"

If the answer is "Yes," then fear has no power over you.

If the answer is "No," then you will be overwhelmed by your fear. You will revert to your old reactive behavior patterns and the world of shame and blame will re-constitute around you.

I hate to tell you this, but there is more than one tiger in your life. One tiger is your negative thinking and the other tiger is your fear, and these tigers seem to have some kind of pact or agreement, because when one tiger is fed, the other one is fed too. Your negativity feeds your fear and your fear feeds your negativity. Mind and emotions are intimately connected.

So now you not only have to stop feeding the tigers, you have to get them on your lap and stroke the back of their necks. You need to tell them that everything is okay the way it is and you will protect them from any harm. It sounds stupid, but when the tigers get enough love and reassurance, they forget that they haven't eaten dinner or lunch.

So we keep asking "What kind of zookeeper are you? When fear arises in consciousness, who is holding it and how is it being held?"

Even when suffering is greatly diminished in our life and we are living in freedom and joy, we still need to do our spiritual practice. Without it, we can easily be drawn back into the drama.

HAPPINESS IS A CHOICE

In each moment, we choose to be happy or to find fault and complain. In the past, this choice was not a very conscious one, so more often than not we were finding fault and complaining about everything that was happening in our lives. But now that we have reached a certain level of awareness, we understand that we are responsible for what we see and how we see it.

That means that we have a choice in every moment whether to accept or resist, bless or curse, complain or be grateful, perceive lack or abundance. That choice is awesome and profound.

A recent study found the Danes the happiest people on planet earth. Closer investigation made it clear that it wasn't because they were more optimistic or resilient than others. The unique gift that they brought to the table was "low expectations." Because they did not expect a lot from life, they could better appreciate all the good things that came their way.

Think of it this way. The German expects a Mercedes. The English expect a Jaguar or a Rolls. The Italian expects a Ferrari. But the Dane is happy with a used Volkswagen. So it isn't surprising that there are more Danes who are happy.

If you lower your expectations, you will be more grateful for every little gift that comes your way. And living in gratitude is one of the greatest pathways to happiness and abundance.

I know I told you I would not give you a prescription, but here is the closest I will come to giving you a tip on creating a happier and more fulfilling life:

- First, lower your expectations.

- Second, be grateful for what you have.

Lowering your expectations opens you up to the possibilities before you. You are more willing to accept reality as it unfolds. Being grateful for what you have and what comes to you raises your vibration and helps you attract more of the same into your life.

Try this and see if it works for you. But do it with heart. If your heart is not in it, if your intention is not there, it will not work.

In the past, when you lived in victim consciousness, you were good at finding all the things you did not like and feeling sorry for yourself. Now it's time to find all the things that you do like and celebrate them.

In the past, you focused on lack and reinforced it, living in poverty and powerlessness. Now it's time to focus on what is fully present and be grateful for it, enabling it to grow and multiply.

In the past, you focused on what was wrong. Now you understand it works better to focus on what's right.

When you spend your time finding fault, you have to live with all the faults that you find. That is a rather silly way to spend your life. It's time to let the faults go and focus on what is wonderful and inspiring.

Whatever you focus on grows and expands. That is the creative power of your mind. If you know that, you realize that dwelling on the negative is the fastest way to trash your life.

On the other hand, focusing on the positive is like bringing fertilizer to the plant. It helps it grow in leaps and bounds.

Find the good, and goodness will surround you. Find the bad and live in a hell of your own making. It is your choice.

STOP LOOKING FOR PAYBACK

I know you think that God is angry at you and is going to punish you. I know you also think that God is angry at your brother for hurting you and is going to punish him too. But what if God isn't interested in punishing anyone, because He knows it doesn't work? What if there is no Divine payback, no punishment, no righteous retribution?

What if God is only interested in love and forgiveness? Then, any energy you put into judging or hating others isn't going to help you. In fact, it is just going to come back and slap you in the face. Is that a game you like to play? Do you still want to trade an eye for an eye, a tooth for a tooth, one murdered child for another? You can spend a lifetime building walls, prisons and concentration camps.

Is that the life you want to lead? If not, give it up. Drop it, cold turkey. The way to heaven has been carefully laid out for you. Just follow it. *Do unto others as you would have them do unto you.* That's it. It's very simple, very practical.

Get off the payback wagon before it blows up in your face. Learn to take baby steps. Learn to walk your talk. The words of love are empty when they are not followed by acts of love.

It's time to make peace with yourself, to make peace with your brother and sister. It's time to make peace with your God. Let's all get on the same page. Then we can move forward out of suffering into joy, freedom, and unconditional love. That is much more fun and it is an activity that is supported by the universe.

CHAPTER EIGHTEEN

Relinquishing the Past

Each day that dawns is unique and brings something new into your life. It might bring a new gift or a new challenge. It might bring both at the same time.

If you dwell on what happened in the past, you will drag the past around with you like a sack of bones. After a while, that sack gets pretty heavy and it becomes a real handicap. It prevents you from being fully present and showing up in a timely way. Opportunities to grow and to change are missed and old dysfunctional patterns are reinforced.

When you don't make the changes in your life that are necessary, your soul gets restless. It doesn't trust your ego structure to run your life. So it makes its own plans, the pressure inside builds up and, without warning, an earthquake is unleashed that forces you to change. This is not an ideal way to operate.

Change is necessary for growth, but calamities are not.

When your house gets cluttered, you move the old Knick knacks and outdated furniture out into the street and have a yard sale. You have to do the same thing with the contents of your consciousness. Take that bag of bones you are carrying around and toss it into the rubbish heap.

Whenever your load gets heavy and the weight of that sack is holding you back, you have to lighten the load. Do this repeatedly and you will stay alert and fully present in your life.

In the Hindu Trinity, the God Shiva is considered by some to be the holiest of the three Gods. Shiva is the God of destruction. He comes to take away what we no longer need so that it does not hold us back. Whenever we have difficulty letting go, Shiva comes in and gives us a helping hand.

No form stays functional forever. Every form degrades and eventually becomes obsolete. This is true for machines, for software, even for bodies. Every form has a useful life. Once it is no longer useful, it needs to be discarded.

Some forms can be reformed, refitted, retooled and their useful life can be extended. Some cannot.

It is always sad when a great athlete stays in the game when he can no longer compete with younger players. Then, we have to watch him slowly fall apart. That can be uncomfortable and embarrassing for him and for us. It would be far better for all of us if he were wise enough to make a graceful exit.

The hermit crab knows when his shell becomes too tight. So he surrenders that shell and finds one that offers him room to grow. He not only cleans house; he changes his house as often as necessary.

The caterpillar knows when his life as an eight legged creature is no longer functional, so he crawls into the cocoon that will transform his life.

Human beings are no different. We need change. Old forms must be retooled or discarded. Our lives do not shine energetically if we do not constantly recharge our batteries or find new challenges.

Jesus told us that we need new skins for new wine. As consciousness ripens and expands, it can no longer be contained by an old lifestyle with dysfunctional patterns of sacrifice and self-betrayal.

A healthy life needs renewal. That is true for body, mind, and spirit. It is true for relationships. That which does not move, change and renew itself becomes brittle and resistant. It cannot stand up to the wind and the waves. The challenges of life become overwhelming. The form cracks open and is swept away in the flood tide.

When we live just to accumulate money and possessions, we become old quickly. Our lives become devoid of energy and purpose. We contract in fear and joy and gratitude are absent from our lives. We may have a lot of money, but we become spiritually bankrupt.

If we are wise, we will seek renewal before it is too late. We will find a way to reconnect with our energy and purpose. We will live not to accumulate worldly possessions but to cultivate and share the treasures within our hearts and minds.

That which does not renew itself meets an early end. Its shelf-life is limited.

That is why Shiva is our friend. Shiva helps us let go of what we no longer need, what has already served its purpose in our lives. Shiva keeps our load light so that we can be fully present in our lives. That means we stay in our creative flow and are constantly renewing ourselves.

We are all afraid to let go, but if we don't let go, we implode. Try taking a breath and not letting go of it and see what happens.

Letting go is what enables us to reach out and receive something new. We let go of the old breath so that we can take a new one. A healthy and resilient life is syncopated by equal parts of inhaling and exhaling. When there is too much inhaling, we become quickly tired and de-energized. That is what happens to most of us. We take in more than we give out.

In order to come back into balance and regain our creative energy, we have to focus on the exhale, on letting go, on giving rather than receiving. When we do that, we are amazed. When we extend energy to others, it comes back tenfold.

Now, instead of sucking energy from others, we have energy coming back to us. We have successfully changed the energetics of our lives.

Now, we just have to keep the cycle of giving and receiving going. When we continue to give as we receive, we have a constant flow of gratitude and abundance in our lives.

ALLOWING THE FUTURE TO UNFOLD

Many people live for the future rewards. They work hard so that they can take an inspiring vacation or so they can send their children to college. There is nothing wrong with planning for the future, as long as you know that the future is unpredictable.

The best laid plans of mice and men do not always come to fruition. That does not mean that you should not plan. It does suggest, however, that if your present is always future-oriented, then you may not be fully present here and now. And when you are not here completely, your power to live in the creative flow is diminished.

If you do not take time to smell the roses now, when will you do it? If you are working 18 hours a day saving for your son's college tuition and are too busy to go to his basketball games, you and he are missing out on something that might be a lot more important than college. After all, your son has only one daddy and if daddy is not there for him, he may go off to college wounded and feeling disconnected from you.

There is no planning for the future that is more important than your capacity to be emotionally present in your life. That means giving quality time to yourself and your family. It means taking time to enjoy the events and circumstances of life as they unfold day by day.

If you are not emotionally present and connected, you may make a lot of money and achieve great social recognition, but you will not be happy. Being happy means that you have a loving relationship with yourself and with others. It has nothing to do with riches, or name and fame.

Unfortunately, one can squander the present by being focused on the future. And then, ironically perhaps, when the future comes it is not satisfying. A better and more congruent plan would be to enjoy the present as intensely as possible and allow the future to unfold.

If you know that you cannot control the outcome, you realize the futility of living for some future gratification that may or may not come. That realization helps you to be more present in your life right now.

If you are present now, then you are connected to an abundant universe whose gifts are constantly being offered to you and to others. You don't have to go out hell-bent to try to make a fortune and manipulate or harm others in the process. Your goal might be great, but it never justifies the means when the means are not charitable to yourself or others.

Having a goal is not really a problem, especially if your goal is heart-felt. The problem is when the means you choose to reach the goal take you away from it, instead of toward it.

For example, your goal may be to go to heaven. But you may believe that you can do so only if you destroy or imprison others who believe in a different God or religion. You choose a sinful path to heaven in the hope that your sins will be forgiven because you had the right God.

When you get to heaven, there are three possible outcomes. The first one — the one you hope is true — is that God forgives you and agrees that your actions were acceptable. The second one — which you don't think about much — is that God tells you that you made a very big mistake and you will have to atone for it for the next fifty lifetimes. And the third one —— Khadra's favorite — is that God even there to greet you, because He opted out of the drama when He gave you free will, in which case you have to live with your guilt and fear of retribution until you are finally able to heal them.

So chances are you are not going to get the results you expect because the path you chose was not congruent with the goal. Only the heavenly path leads to heaven. Only the path of love, kindness, forgiveness leads us to the place beyond sin. No other path can lead there.

If the means are not consistent with the goal, then the goal will not be reached. That is why there is so much misunderstanding and misery in this world. Our goals sound great, but the means that we choose to reach our goals are full of manipulation and trespass.

If we want peace on earth, we must choose the path of peace. That path unfolds in each moment. And the choice that you or I make right now is consequential. If we don't choose peace now, it will not come to pass in the future.

Yes, the future will unfold, but we must do our part. If we put off wise and necessary actions today, it may be too late to take them in the future. Global warming did not happen overnight. It happened moment by moment, one choice and one person at a time.

We have to realize that each moment asks us to make a wise and compassionate choice. Each moment offers us a new present and the beginning of a new chain of events. But we will have to build the chain, one link at a time, one moment at a time.

This is the amazing gift that the universe has given us: the choice to create anew in each moment. Although we cannot predict or control the future, what happens depends in many respects on the choices that we make here and now.

The past is gone. The future has not occurred. Now is the only time we have. Let us do our best to be emotionally present and to make wise and compassionate choices.

CHAPTER NINETEEN

Amazing Grace

A new world is being born today as each one of us lives in trust and does the best that s/he can. There is nothing magical or glamorous about this. There are no signs that promise redemption or success. There is just your consciousness and mine and the choices that we make in each moment.

Can we be truly present and alert in our lives? Can we live in compassionate awareness, celebrating our affinities and respecting our differences?

Can we give up shame and blame, stop attacking each other and make amends when we trespass? Can we turn the other cheek and offer each other understanding and forgiveness?

If we can, the earth will move differently under our feet, and we will be walking a different path from the one we have trod in the past.

It is true that the jury is out. We do not know the outcome. But we do know we have a choice to make right now.

Beyond that, we cannot speculate, nor can we give the world some meaning that it does not have.

This world is an experiment. We came here for one purpose only: to learn to love ourselves and to pass that love on to all the other human beings who share our experience.

Regardless of whether we learn our collective lessons, each individual must pursue the path toward his own awakening and redemption.

Each one of us chose to be here. We chose to accept the gift of Free Will that God gave to us. Now it is up to us to begin to shine the light within us so that we can heal and become an instrument for the healing of others.

To be sure, salvation will not come to our world unless it begins in our own hearts and minds. We are the bringers of love to our own experience. As we bring it, the light within begins to shine, illuminating the inner and outer worlds.

There are many powerful stories of healing and redemption that can inspire us. One was documented in a song written by the captain of a slave ship who had his own powerful experience of forgiveness. It is a song that lives close to our hearts, for it could have been written for you or for me:

> Amazing Grace, How Sweet the Sound,
> To save a wretch like me.
> I once was lost, but now am found.
> Was blind, but now I see.

The song celebrates the triumph of love over fear. It celebrates the fact that we can have a change of heart and a change of purpose. We can stop being a victim or a victimizer and instead be the instrument of love in a world that is starving for it. Yes, one man or woman can answer the call and make a difference. Those who have the courage to change bring the light not just for themselves, but for all of us.

Let us be honest. Being a human being is not easy. It is fraught with difficulties and challenges.

The life of any human being is filled with mistakes, some of them grievous ones. There is a lot that each one of us must atone for. As Jesus knew, we need forgiveness as much as we need our daily bread, and maybe more.

Without forgiveness, we are all condemned to die on the cross, both victims and victimizers.

But the extraordinary truth is that each one of us can forgive and be forgiven. Each one of us can undo the hell s/he has made. Each one of us can put down our cross and begin the long journey of creating a peaceful heart and a peaceful world.

The fact that any one of us could wake up — be it Jesus, or Buddha, or the slave ship owner —— demonstrates that the capacity for awakening lives inside of us and the promise of forgiveness is not given just to other men and women. It is also given to us.

SPIRITUAL PRACTICE

Heaven is not in the sky above. Heaven is in our hearts. When we are connected to love in our hearts, we are in alignment with the truth.

Some of us have difficulty stilling the restless voices of our minds and coming into our hearts. That is why yoga or meditation can be helpful. When the mind slows down and vibrates with the heart, our consciousness expands. We move out of monkey mind into a state of pure awareness in which our inner truth can be heard.

Of course, we do not necessarily stay in this consciousness. As soon as we move out into the world and begin to listen to the ideas and expectations of others, we are thrown off-center. Things become muddled and confused again.

So we have to understand that our vibration has been diminished and that anything that we do now will not be helpful. We have to realize that it is time to go back into our inner sanctuary and recharge.

Going within will not be effective if it is something that we do once a month. It takes only a day and sometimes less than a day for our energy to be drained and our clarity to be compromised. So whenever that happens, we know that it is time for us to re-engage in our spiritual practice.

In the Workbook of *A Course in Miracles* we are asked to take five minutes out of every hour to go within. That can be very powerful! It reminds us that self-awareness is necessary throughout the day.

Of course, whatever it is, our spiritual practice must be done joyfully and with heart. The practice itself must always be its own reward, not just a means toward an end.

To be sure, consistent practice does bring results. The more connected you are to love in your heart, the easier it is for you to stay centered and be your authentic self in the world. You are energetically stronger, and less likely to betray yourself or give your power away.

THE PROOF IS IN THE PUDDING

The proof is always in the pudding. If you don't eat the pudding you are not going to taste the fruit.

Reading any book, including this one, is not going to wake you up. Waking up depends on you and the choices that you make.

Your choices create your own unique path of awakening. It won't look like anyone else's path and it really shouldn't.

Spiritual teachings are not meant to create a new dogma that you must swallow and parrot to others. They are designed to take you into your heart, to connect you to the source of love and the wellspring of truth.

Once you are connected, you are guided from within.

Every path has impediments and obstacles. There are always lessons to learn and some of them must be learned again and again. The more you resist the truth, the more you delay your journey.

Be a willing learner and you will move through your pain. Patience and compassion with yourself will lighten your load and soften the rocky ground under your feet. What you bring to the journey — whether humility or hubris, trust or blame — will shape your path and its degree of difficulty.

That would be true of any path you follow.

You can waste a lifetime changing teachers and paths, going around in circles, like a cat chasing its own tail. In the end, it's helpful to settle down and put one foot in front of the other.

If you do that, your arrival is guaranteed. It is just a matter of time before you get there.

In the end, Job was rewarded for showing up and doing his spiritual practice. How could he not be? In the face of incredible odds, he stood his ground. He remained faithful to himself and his God. When all was said and done, only good things remained in Job's life. All that had been given and taken away from him was restored in even greater measure.

When we do our best, when we stand our ground, when we live with courage and faith, the universe answers in kind. While the Rabbi was certainly right that sometimes "bad things happen to good people," it is also true that "good things happen to good people."

In the final analysis, only goodness prevails. That is the grace of God. No matter what we do, no matter how many mistakes we make, no matter how little we feel that we deserve, God does not withhold from us Her blessings or Her love.

The God of love forgives us and showers us with grace and abundance. Even when we turn away from Him, His love for us remains steadfast.

The child may be angry at the parent. She may even reject the parent's love. But the parent does not stop loving the child. The parent's love for the child is eternal and unchangeable.

You and I are the children of a loving God. Wherever we go, God's love goes with us. There is never a time or a place where that love is absent.

In our hearts we know this and in time we begin to trust it.

That is why David was not afraid to stand up against Goliath. Even as a boy he knew that God was with him. Even as a boy he knew "The Lord is my Shepherd."

The Lord is our shepherd too. He guides us out of bondage and out of suffering. He leads us to the promised land. That is why I say to you now "May God be with you."

May the love of God live in your heart.
May the peace of God live in your mind.
May the presence of God abide with you.
May Her grace surround you.
And may Her blessings be with you
all the days of your life,
now and forevermore.

Namaste.

IMAGES

page 6 *Riverbank of Peach Blossoms*, Shitao

pages 21, 57, 91, 109, 135
Early Autumn, details, Qian Kuan

page 45 *Butterfly*, Annick vom Kolk

page 63 *Horses*, Xu Beihong

page 106 from *Five Bulls*, Han Huang

page 136 *Tigers*, Liu Jiyou

page 158 *Plum Blossoms, detail*, Qi Baishi

Paul Ferrini is the author of 50 books on love, healing and forgiveness. His unique blend of spirituality and psychology goes beyond self-help and recovery into the heart of healing. His conferences, retreats, and *Affinity Group Process* have helped thousands of people deepen their practice of forgiveness and open their hearts to the divine presence in themselves and others.

For more information on Paul Ferrini's work, visit his website at www.paulferrini.com or www.lightforthesoul.com. The website has many excerpts from Paul's books, as well as information on his workshops and retreats. Be sure to request Paul's email newsletter, his daily wisdom message, as well as a free catalog of his books and audio products. You can also email us at orders@heartwayspress.com or call us at 941-776-8001.

BOOKS BY PAUL FERRINI

To order or learn more, go to
www.paulferrini.com
or **www.lightforthesoul.com**

HEALING BOOKS

Light for the Soul
Answering the Call of the Soul
Having the Time of Your Life
Healing Your Life
The Keys to the Kingdom
Real Happiness
Real Happiness, the Workbook
Embracing Our True Self
The Hidden Jewel
The Laws of Love
The Power of Love
The Presence of Love

RELATIONSHIP BOOKS

When Love Comes as a Gift
Dancing with the Beloved
Creating a Spiritual Relationship
Living in the Heart
Crossing the Water (Poetry)

FORGIVENESS BOOKS

The Twelve Steps of Forgiveness
The Wounded Child's Journey
Bridge to Reality
From Ego to Self
The Wisdom of the Self